WAVES OF GRIEF

Devotionals of HOPE for Widows

A Widow's Might, Inc.

www.awidowsmight.org

Visit the website at www.awidowsmight.org

Printed in the United States of America

ISBN- 9781075936548

CONTENTS

Section 1: What You Can Expect

Becoming a widow is one of the hardest challenges we will ever face. But we are not alone – God is with us!

At first, the waves of grief are so huge and so overwhelming, we are left sputtering for breath, wondering how we will ever survive.

Eventually, we learn to ride the waves.

It may seem hard to imagine, but even now God is weaving blessings from what you are going through.

In Section 1, our devotionals are focused primarily on what you may experience in the grief journey and how God will be with you along the way.

We hope that by sharing our experiences you will not feel so alone and that you will become more aware of God's faithfulness in your own journey.

THE ROCKS KEEP COMING
by Elizabeth Dyer Colvard

Twice in one week I heard the same story from completely different sources. One was from the pulpit at my church and the other was on the Christian music station I have been playing in my house. I couldn't help but imagine this story relates to us as widows perfectly.

A little boy was playing with his toy sailboat on the shore of a quiet lake. When the wind pulled the sail boat away from the shoreline, he began to cry as it went farther and farther away.

His older brother came upon the scene and began throwing stones at his tiny boat. The young boy cried, "Why are you throwing stones at my boat?"

The brother said, "I'm throwing stones on the FAR side of your boat to create some waves to bring the sailboat BACK to you. Trust me; I know what I'm doing."

Did you read that? "Trust me, I know what I'm doing." Does that hit you like it hits me? The little boat is my life. As I was busy living, I never noticed how I had begun to feel entitled. Trusting God was fairly easy while I was comfortable. I bobbled around in the warm waters, saying all the right things and living the right way. I knew the verses which included:

Trust in the Lord with all your heart, and do not lean on your own understanding. Proverbs 3:5 ESV

And then the bottom fell out. Widowhood was one of the many "rocks" that were coming at me. And like the small boy in the story, I shouted at God, "Stop throwing rocks at my life!" "I can't take any more!" "Are you trying to destroy me?"

Charles Spurgeon, a famous Bible teacher and author from the 19th century, struggled with depression and painful diseases. He has many quotes you can find online that are as true today as they were a hundred years ago.

One is this:

"I have learned to kiss the waves that throw me up against the Rock of Ages."

Kiss the waves.

I just love that phrase. It doesn't mean some crass, sarcastic kissing. I believe it is more like embracing. Accepting.

It is a different way to express the acceptance of Romans 8:28. The Amplified says it this way:
And we know [with great confidence] that God [who is deeply concerned about us] causes all things to work together [as a plan] for good for those who love God, to those who are called according to His plan and purpose.

Those rocks that send waves our direction, they have a purpose. They push us closer to God, our anchor in the storms of life. Those trials, those difficulties, those battles with sin. They push us into the arms of the One Who loves us.

What is the alternative? The alternative is to fight against the waves and push away from the ripples that are drawing us to God. Trust me when I say, I KNOW that way is exhausting and a complete waste. I know, because I fought the waves for too long. The fighting just pulled me away from God and His loving arms. I couldn't accept that He loved me when the rocks of life kept hitting me. Marriage crisis. Health decline. Broken relationships. Financial collapse. Death. Widowhood. I was rowing my little boat as hard as I could my own way, in my own strength. And I got nowhere.

We pray that A Widow's Might ministry can assist you in drawing closer to the Rock of Ages. Let's stop fighting against those waves and embrace that God wants to draw us to Himself.

Almighty Father, thank You for the love and care You have for us. When the storms of life rock our worlds, help us, guide us, hold us. Keep us from fighting against the difficulties and fully trust You. Amen

My thoughts:

_____

_____

_____

_____

_____

_____

_____

_____

_____

_____

_____

_____

_____

_____

_____

_____

_____

_____

_____

_____

_____

_____

_____

_____

_____

△ △ △

GRIEF IS A FICKLE FRIEND
by Jennifer Stanton Boswell

"Fear not, for I am with you; Be not dismayed, for I am your God. I will strengthen you. Yes, I will help you, I will uphold you with My righteous right hand." Isaiah 41:10 (NKJV)

It happened again, on a Tuesday, about a week ago. I was driving to work, dressed and ready, makeup on, prepared to conquer the day. Being a freelance writer, I usually only go into the office on Tuesdays. I was stopped at a red light, and my late husband Michael's favorite song played on the radio – Whom Shall I Fear by Chris Tomlin.

The first several months after his death, I would break down every time I heard the song. Now, usually, I can listen to it with a thankful heart. But that day, that Tuesday, it hit me – the extreme wave of grief – catching me off guard.

I sat at the light, tears pouring down, trying to pull myself together. I was just five minutes away from the office. "Of all days," I thought, "I do not want to be late, and I can't go in there in tears. It's been more than two-and-a-half years. I can't be this upset; no one will understand."

But the truth is, we can be. Grief is a fickle friend and doesn't just go away when we hit the one-year mark, or two-year or 10-year marks. We never "get over it." Grief shows up whenever she feels like it — at work, with a client, the grocery store, your child's sporting event and so on. And, whether it's been five weeks or five years since the loss of your beloved, it still happens, and that is our reality.

Though this journey is long and treacherous, with unexpected twists and turns, with the Lord's strength and comfort, it gets better, and joy can still be found. The grief and sadness we have from the loss of our husbands will never go away, but that all-consuming sorrow will, if we let Jesus in.

"You have turned for me my mourning into dancing; You have put off my sackcloth and clothed me with gladness, to the end that my glory may sing praise to You and not be silent. O Lord my God, I will give thanks to You forever." Psalm 30:11-12 (NKJV)

Today, though I miss Michael every day, that all–consuming, paralyzing grief comes on days and moments that are fewer and farther between. And when they do come, I know that the Lord will be there, arms wide open, to comfort, and give peace and strength. He is the reason I've come this far, and though circumstances can be difficult to understand, I KNOW He will uphold me and never let me down.

The Lord never promised a life without pain, but He did promise to be by our side every step of the way.

"When you go through deep waters, I will be with you. When you go through rivers of difficulty, you will not drown. When you walk through the fire of oppression, you will not be burned up; the flames will not consume you." Isaiah 43:2 (NLV)

Lord, remind us to rely on Your strength, not our own. It is the only way we can step forward in this life 'after'. Guide us through the valleys, and help us be at peace when joy comes our way. Thank You for Your faithfulness through it all. Amen.

My thoughts:

_____

_____

_____

_____

_____

_____

_____

_____

_____

_____

_____

_____

_____

_____

_____

_____

_____

_____

_____

_____

_____

_____

_____

_____

△ △ △

WHAT SHALL WE DO?
By Janene Preston Gaynor

"Teacher, what shall we do?"- Luke 3:12 (ESV)

What a great question! Countless times I have asked this very same question.

While my husband was alive, he and I made up a happy we. I know I have changed since my beloved died, and I wistfully recall the pre-widow me. Although fundamentally me, I am not the same. Some changes are probably permanent and others temporary, but during the waves of grief I now realize God was teaching me and answering that question.

Here are some examples.
- Treasure those I love more than ever.
- See how fragile life is and how it can change in a heartbeat.
- Appreciate the eternal destination we have in Christ more than ever!

- While I'm likely to isolate when my pain is high, I've learned to balance staying connected with others.
- I have felt the cradling of prayers and want others to experience this.
- Relate to God's desire to have a relationship with us, because relational separation is painful and eternal separation I cannot conceive.
- I have seen great kindness and support from my Christian community and felt God's love through them.
- Widow's brain has required I extend grace to myself, which I extend also to those at a loss on what to say or not say.
- I am less light-hearted but more tender-hearted.
- Protect my emotional reserves before it vaporizes.
- I have also known joy and learned new skills, and slayed giants as a widow. God has made new things possible I could not have imagined.
- Most assuredly, I know God as my Rock. More than ever.

Perhaps some of these points have struck a chord with you. What would be on your list?

The impact of the death of a spouse cannot help but to change us. Even so, with God on our side, He adds new facets to our understanding as He gently guides us. Most of the points I list were taught without even registering at the time. Yet, God knew the question, "What do I do, God?" has been a constant refrain in my heart, even when my mind was in a widow's fog. My tears were prayers and so are yours.

We have an amazingly good God, who is more perfectly diligent in attention for our best than we know how to be.

Please join me in prayer to Him now:
Precious God of the Universe, our Creator, our Savior, our Lord, thank You that we are eternally Your's through Christ. Thank You for every facet You add to us as you so lovingly guide and instruct us, especially at times of great sorrow and pain. Thank You forever, dear Jesus! Amen

My thoughts:

△ △ △

OTHER SIDE OF THE SOB
by Ami Atkins Wickiser

I watched her greet person after person, carried along by evident grace. She wanted it to be a celebration instead of a funeral. And indeed, the atmosphere buzzed with the hum of conversation while folks enjoyed dinner and dessert. Pictures of a life well-lived filled the space.

From across the room, her eye caught mine. And in the span of a heartbeat, she was in my arms collapsing under the weight of her sobs. Without words, we stood that way for a long time. I held her tightly and cried with her.

"I know I can let it all out with you."

Yes, dear one. It's ok to weep and grieve even amid a celebration of life.

Three years earlier, the same lady was at the hospital when my life shattered, and I collapsed into her arms. We had been alone in the emergency room, Jon and I. But he went into cardiac arrest, and I needed someone to come. Looking down at my phone, there was her contact information. Mechanically, I touched the screen, not completely aware of who I was calling.

She was there when I finally gave a doctor permission to stop trying to save my husband's life. It was in her arms that I silently prayed, "Yes Lord, He's yours. I give him back to you."

Two lives intertwined through the deepest of moments.

But now I was on the other side of the sob.

I can't say I was fully prepared to dive down deep with her, or that her weeping didn't recreate a dozen vivid images in my mind. And I can't say I expected she would let her composure crack and the waves overtake her. But I'm glad she did. For there was grace for her to greet person after person.

And there was grace to weep.

I'm thankful she felt totally safe. And I'm thankful I could share the weeping with her.

On the other side of the sob I realize a few things:

- I know suffering so that I may be able to suffer with others.
- I know redemption in the midst and on the other side of the storm.
- I have been deeply comforted.

Praise God for beauty out of ashes.

His plans and purposes are immensely beautiful.

Blessed be the God and Father of our Lord Jesus Christ, the Father of mercies and God of all comfort, who comforts us in all our affliction, so that we may be able to comfort those who are in any affliction, with the comfort with which we ourselves are comforted by God. For as we share abundantly in Christ's sufferings, so through Christ we share abundantly in comfort too. 2 Corinthians 1:3-5 esv

My thoughts:

_____

_____

_____

_____

_____

_____

_____

_____

_____

_____

_____

_____

_____

_____

_____

_____

_____

_____

_____

△ △ △

IN STEADFAST LOVE, GIVE ME LOVE
by Terri Oxner Sharp

Blessed be the God and Father of our Lord Jesus Christ, the Father of mercies and God of all comfort, who comforts us in all our affliction, so that we may be able to comfort those who are in any affliction, with the comfort with which we ourselves are comforted by God. For as we share abundantly in Christ's sufferings, so through Christ we share abundantly in comfort too. 2 Corinthians 1:3-5 ESV

Comfort. It is the result of resting in God's sovereignty and loving rule over my life.

Peace. I'm not free from troubles, but I possess a profound sense of well-being because God is in control. The one who collapsed, could uphold another. I could look her in the eye and say:

It's ok to weep. It's ok to ask questions.
Cling to Christ. He carries.

"You won't believe me now, but one day it will be better. It may be a long time, but one day you'll want to live again."

Jesus turns suffering into unspeakable joy.

"In your steadfast love give me life, that I may keep the testimonies of your mouth."
Psalm 119:88 (ESV)

The waves of grief crash over my heart. I groan in the agony of distress; then just as quickly peace washes over my soul but a longing for HOME remains there. Oh, have mercy on me, Dear Lord! My heart is torn open and I feel numb! Nothing seems to mean anything...

> The family on the beach is unaware of what I see as I sit here on my ninth floor balcony. A mother laughingly videos daddy holding their little girl's hand as the pair walk away from her. "HOLD ON TIGHT!" I want to scream at them. Now, the daddy is filming the mother and daughter as they walk away, alone. Will they one day walk by themselves again, without him because they have no choice? Will their hearts break as they watch another family video on the beach? Will this pain I feel ever go away? How can the world keep turning and life for everyone just be normal? My life seemingly ended on April 20, 2012; yet I am still stuck here,

supposed to carry on...how? By Your strength and Your steadfast love alone, Lord.

The above is taken from a piece of paper that has been in my Bible since May 8, 2012. It was written just two weeks after my husband's sudden death. Our family was blessed with a trip to the beach to help us process our grief. This paper remains nestled between two pages of Psalm 119, where I was studying during that time. It is a reminder to me of how far the Lord has carried me since that time.

It has been almost five years since my first husband died, and never once did God leave me or forsake me.

That sunny morning He gave me just the first of many reminders that His strength alone would carry me through the worst of times. My mind and heart were screaming in pain, but He gently took me back to where He wanted me to remain, enfolded in His arms and constantly in His Word. He has been so gracious to provide just what I needed each day to help me grow in my love and trust for Him over the years. Now He has blessed me with another man to call my husband; but I never want to forget how God provided strength and comfort to me right from the beginning of my widow journey. I leave this paper reminder in my Bible so that I will tangibly touch both my grief and my confidence in God whenever I turn to that passage of Scripture.

Sisters, God's love is STEADFAST. In our lives as widows it may seem that everything is topsy-turvy and that nothing is steady or trustworthy. But we know from Scripture that God's love is ALWAYS steady and reliable when our world is crashing down around us.

I encourage you to meditate on Psalm 119 if you have never done so. It is long, but taken in pieces, it can be a balm to the hurting, weary soul. I pray that you will allow God to bathe you in His words of comfort and to give you the heart knowledge of His steadfast love today as you go with me to Psalm 119:81-88.

"My soul longs for your salvation; I hope in your word. My eyes long for your promise; I ask, When will you comfort me? For I have become like a wineskin in the smoke, yet I have not forgotten your statutes. How long must your servant endure? When will you judge those who persecute me? The insolent have dug pitfalls for me; they do not live according to your law. All your commandments are sure; they persecute me with falsehood; help me! They have almost

made an end of me on earth, but I have not forsaken your precepts. In your steadfast love give me life, that I may keep the testimonies of your mouth." Psalm 119:81-88 (ESV)

Father, today I pray that we will be strengthened and overwhelmed with Your steadfast love that leads to life in the midst of turmoil! I pray that it will be so real to us that we want to share You with everyone around us today and every day. Amen

My thoughts:

_____

_____

_____

_____

_____

_____

_____

_____

_____

_____

_____

△ △ △

WHAT WILL TOMORROW BRING?
by Sheryl Pepple

Make me to know your ways, O LORD; teach me your paths.
Psalm 25:4 ESV

You never know what tomorrow will bring.

The biggest shock of my life was when the State Troopers showed up at my door to tell me my husband had been killed. Just a few hours before, I had gone to lunch with my husband and had been laughing and joking with him before gently kissing him goodbye as he left on his trip. I never dreamed it would be our last kiss or the last time I would see him on this earth.

I never dreamed of all the horror that would unfold over the next few weeks, months, years. Or to what depth and length I would feel the excruciating, never-ending pain.

I also never dreamed that through it all I would be able to praise God. But I did, and I continue to do so, because God is Lord of my life. And I am so very grateful God is who He says He is.

It has been said that at the root of all sin is pride. We want to do things our way. Never has that been as apparent to me in my own life as it has been since my whole world was turned upside down with my husband's death. At first, I clung to the way things had been and when I couldn't do that anymore, I tried creating my new path. Neither option yielded the right path.

Last week a reader captured the quintessential essence of widowhood in two words, "What now?"

We know tomorrow is coming, but we don't know what to do. We need to know where we are going and how we are going to get there.

A few months ago, I took my grandson with me as I ran some errands. One of my errands included taking some old paint to the recycling center. I had never been to the recycling plant before but with GPS I am fearless these days. Off we went. The journey ended up being way longer than I anticipated because of detours. My frustration level rose quickly. Fortunately, my grandson (who just turned 5) took it all in stride. He carefully watched for signs along the way and asked a few questions, but mostly just sat back and trusted me to lead.

"What now" we ask. "How am I supposed to move forward?" "What will tomorrow bring?" Instead let us pray as David prayed in Psalm 25:4 "Make me to know your ways, O LORD; teach me your paths."

And just like my grandson responded on our journey to the recycling plant, we need to watch for signs along the way and trust that He will lead us. I may not know what tomorrow will bring but I do know who needs to lead the way.

Dear Heavenly Father, we praise You that You are who You say You are! We are grateful we can rejoice and trust in this truth. Thank You, Father, for guiding us, loving us, and protecting us, even when we don't know what tomorrow will bring. Please help us to know Your ways and teach us Your paths. For Your honor and glory. Amen.

My thoughts:

_____

_____

_____

_____

_____

_____

_____

_____

_____

_____

_____

_____

_____

_____

_____

_____

_____

_____

_____

_____

_____

△ △ △

ACCEPTING NO
by Lori Reynolds Streller

Yours, O Lord, is the greatness and the power and the glory and the victory and the majesty, for all that is in the heavens and in the earth is yours. Yours is the kingdom, O Lord, and you are exalted as the head above all.

1 Chronicles 29:11 (ESV)

May I share a secret with you?

Sometimes I get tired of hearing the "feel good" narratives...even from the Christian community.

So often the stories told are ones of victory. Stories where people prayed for years and God granted them their request. I have those in my own life too; years of prayer where God eventually said, "Yes." Our children are a result of such prayers through years of failed adoptions and infertility. I am grateful. But guess what?

I also have stories of years of prayer where God said, "No."

Why don't we hear more of those?

Why are those stories not shared as beautiful tapestries of immense faith as well?

I'd love for someone to share how their life fell apart and they fought to still keep their eyes on Jesus, right in the midst of the chaos and yuck. How they don't know the "why" and they don't see the reason for their loss or pain. That it doesn't feel at all like God "chose" this outcome for the good of anyone, yet they still trust He will make good from it for eternal purposes.

I want to raise my hand and shake my head in affirmative solidarity that THIS STINKS and know that it is okay to hate the situation yet still adore God. That it is normal to have to work hard at finding the joy in all circumstances we are commanded to have; a discipline of joy rather than a natural response.

I guess I selfishly want to know someone else thinks they got totally cheated, that this isn't fair. I want to not be handed a blanket of "it's for the best" when I have two children in this home being raised without their daddy who was madly in love with them.

I guess my whole point to this thought pattern is...it is okay. We don't have to have it all figured out in our accepting no from God.

Life doesn't have to tie up in a pretty bow for it to have meaning and depth.

Our faith isn't less than someone who received an answer of "yes". As a matter of fact, having lived through both "yes" and "no's", I'd have to say in my personal case, my faith is stronger from the "no" journey than it was from the "yes".

I recently heard a question on the radio.
"Do you believe God is in control?"

I repeated it aloud to myself. Really stopping to question, do I believe God is in control of ALL when Tim still died a horrendous death from cancer? A death that God could have prevented, but chose not to; a death that ripped the hearts of many people (but especially the three of us) to shreds in grief...do I believe God is in control of THAT?

I turned off the radio and drove in silence.
Yes.

Yes, I do believe God is in control. I believe He has the power to do anything He desires. He is in control but He is not a controlling God. There is a difference. His eye is on eternity. He is faithful. On this earth we are guaranteed struggles and pain. One of their purposes is to draw us closer to Him and to direct our focus to eternity.

So here I stand, sharing my "No" story and still raising my hands in honor to the God who is in control; the Faithful One who doesn't equate my faith with an earthly happy ending, but instead equates it with the blessing of knowing Him better.

Father God, it is extremely possible that I will never understand the "No" answers this side of heaven, but I still call upon Your name as Faithful. Thank You that You are less concerned with my desire to have all the answers and are more concerned with my eternal relationship with You. I trust You even when I don't like the answers. My story is no less relevant than stories with "yes's". Amen.

My thoughts:

_____

_____

_____

_____

_____

_____

_____

_____

_____

_____

_____

_____

_____

_____

_____

_____

_____

_____

_____

_____

_____

_____

_____

△ △ △

WHITE OUT FAITH
by Jill Byard

She is not afraid of snow for her household, for all her household are clothed with scarlet. Proverbs 31:21 ESV

White on white, set in a background of more white, throw in a steady wind, temperatures below zero and you have the makings of a good ol' northern winter blizzard. I found myself smack in the middle of this scenario during a six-hour road trip. Two hours away from home and the visibility was almost non-existent; turning around wasn't safe. I was feeling extremely anxious about what I was going to encounter as I kept moving ever so slowly forward. The only thing I knew for sure was I had to move, that sitting still wasn't safe. So, I called out in my uncertainty "Lord, please protect us on our travels. Help us!"

As I was inching along the snowy stretch of highway, I realized there was a spiritual lesson about my journey in grief in the midst of the whiteout swirling around me.

While in the midst of this long whiteout-when I realized that it wasn't even safe to turn around and go back the way I had come-I realized that I would have to go straight through it, and that slowly was probably the safest way to proceed. I couldn't just stop moving or turn around. And that's how it is with grief. We do not want to walk through it, but we must. We can't turn back because it's not healthy. The safest way is to keep moving forward.

The long day of traveling in blizzard conditions made my eyes hurt. I kept straining them to try and catch a glimpse of what was ahead, but it was impossible because the white was all around me. If I thought about what was ahead, I would worry more. I had to stay focused on the moment, focused on the present. I had to seize it in order to keep making progress. So it is with the future and my grief journey. The further out into the future I look, the harder it is to find peace. It's overwhelming that I definitely can't see up ahead, around curves, or over hills. But I have to stop worrying about what is too far ahead and focus on the right now. I have to trust that as I move further in my journey, He will continue to equip me with the skills I will need to get around the curves or to the top of the hills.

As I kept moving down the road, it was difficult to even detect where exactly the road was. I began relying on the rumble strips or chatter bumps to help guide me in my lane.

I am so thankful that God is even better than those rumble strips or chatter bumps on this grief road. Sometimes when grief swirls around me and I am smack in the middle of one of its whiteouts, His voice, and His truth guide me like the rumble strips encouraging me to keep moving forward no matter the pace. He sees what is beyond the now and He has it covered. Chatting with Jesus out loud or to myself helps keep me stay in the center. It was a necessity as I was traveling and it is a complete necessity as I make my way through the storms on this grief journey. My traveling would be even slower if I ventured out on my own. I know, I have tried it and I end up in a bank of deep despair that will need more than a tow truck to get me out.

Dear Lord, Please help us to cry out to You in the midst of our grief. Help us to remember to cling to the knowledge You have our future in the palm of Your hand. We thank You for the work You are going to do on our behalf in our present and our future. You are great and worthy to be praised. In Your Mighty Name, Amen.

My thoughts:

_____

_____

_____

_____

_____

_____

_____

_____

_____

_____

_____

_____

_____

_____

_____

_____

_____

_____

_____

△ △ △

PACKING UP YOUR SORROWS
by Bonnie Vickers

"For My yoke is easy, and My burden is light."
Matthew 11:30 (ESV)

It has been said that there is an "art to packing" successfully. Many would reason that effective packing means taking all you need while keeping the load light. I know the "packing" drill oh so well, as I have been a flight attendant for over thirty years now and traveling is a big part of my life. I have packed a suitcase more times than I care to count and can truthfully say I have mastered the art of effective packing.

To make a trip successful, what we decide to place in our luggage is extremely important! A personal trip this past week made me think just how much this is like our life. It is really important to guard what we place in our personal luggage – our heart.

As I have walked through this grief journey of losing someone who was such a vital part of my life on earth, I have struggled with what I now place in my luggage. Sorrow. Fear. Anger. Doubt. Loneliness. Oh, and did I mention sorrow? You get the picture. These are heavy emotions. They weigh me down and take up space that does not allow me to be an effective tool in serving God. If we allow it, sorrow can be devastating. But, trust me when I say, God means for the sorrow to do great things. We will become more effective in our Christian walk than we would have been without the sorrow, IF, and only if, we allow Him to use us and our story to minister to others. Ministering to others does not necessarily have to be in the form of writing or speaking, but simply how we live through the sorrow, Praising Him even in the storm.

Eventually, we will be able to pack away the sorrow and allow God room in our luggage to open the rivers of His grace. To do any less would be a great disservice to Him. Our load is lightened as we let go of the heaviness that sorrow, fear, anger, doubt and loneliness place in our heart. And, oh my friend, how He wants to help.

All who willingly come will receive peace and comfort in their heart. We must take His yoke and submit to His authority. He desires to accept the willing servant and it is here we can find rest for our soul. This is Christ's invitation to join with us and carry our load. We must come to Him daily for deliverance from all the heaviness this world offers.

Heavenly Father,   Thank You for emotions, even the emotion of sorrow, Lord. As hard as this grief journey of losing our beloved husband is, we ask You to come with us to help carry the burden. We pray that others can see the hope we have in You. I pray for all of my widowed sisters on this journey, Lord. Give them strength as they begin to pack away their sorrow and replace it with joy. Amen

My thoughts:

_____

_____

_____

_____

_____

_____

_____

_____

_____

_____

△ △ △

Section 2: God's Love

If there is one thing
We must remember
above all else
it is
that God is Love.
It is His very nature.
Everything we go through
is filtered
through His love.

LOVE'S ETERNAL ORIGIN
by Janene Preston Gaynor

"We love because He first loved us."– 1 John 4:19 (ESV)

My love for my husband did not die with him. I bet you can say the same thing about your husband, and there is a good reason for that!

Real love, the giving kind, reflects the nature of God. "God is Love," and He created us in His image. (1 John 4:8, Gen. 1:27)

Love has an eternal origin. The very fact we grieve mirrors the love we carry beyond our husband's deaths.

We miss.
We regret.
We long.

We grieve because LOVE acutely feels death's forced separation. My husband was my better half. It would not be an exaggeration to say for a good while I felt amputated, incomplete, and my life a dismembered place. I experienced the conflict of hating that my beloved was gone but also not wanting him with me to continue suffering.

No wonder Jesus came because the agony of separation from a loved one is abhorrent—totally unacceptable and an offense to love. God did not want that eternal distance—like a vast ocean of darkness to get between us. He wanted us close and that's what love wants... to be close.

Because of love's eternal origin, death separated me from my husband but cannot separate me from my love for him. While the eternal origin of love shines in this, grieving is incredibly painful, complex, and layered. Triggers, like land mines, lay in wait for us.

While, "never again" thoughts are triggered by countless associations, very intensely at first, acknowledging and talking with God about them helped. What didn't help was dwelling on them. If I did, it was like digging a pit and jumping in. Grieving is difficult enough without that!

Despite the pain and sorrow now, never would I have missed the love and tapestry of our lives together.

You and I know who and what we miss, but what future good do we anticipate? Future plans with my husband were banished in the instant he exhaled his last breath. However, "we walk by faith, not by sight," 2 Corinthians. 5;7 (ESV).

Eyes of FAITH are crucial to move forward and faith needs to nestle into Truth.

"Who shall separate us from the love of Christ? Shall tribulation, or distress, or persecution, or famine, or nakedness, or danger, or sword? No, in all these things we are more than conquerors through him who loved us. For I am sure that neither death nor life, nor angels nor rulers, nor things present nor things to come, nor powers, nor height nor depth, nor anything else in all creation, will be able to separate us from the love of God in Christ Jesus our Lord." - Rms. 8:35, 37-39 (ESV)

As widows, we share an experience and understanding. Life as we knew it changed instantly. Yet, while life has altered so much, it is comforting that:
The future holds the promise of God's love, tomorrow and always. God's love is never-ending, never-changing, and forever true. Faith is our secure anchor into His love and a sacred place to exhale.

Lord God, thank You that we love because You first loved us. Whether our hearts feel battered, parched, numb, or tentative, meet us there and refuel us with Your love. We are created to love You and one another. Use us still, for the world needs nothing more than Your healing love. Thank You, that we are able to cherish love for our husbands as a true gift from You, Lord Jesus. Amen

My thoughts:

_____

_____

_____

_____

_____

_____

_____

_____

_____

△ △ △

DWELL IN MY LOVE
by Jill Byard

Dwell in Me, and I will dwell in you. John 15:4 AMP

Ever need to feel relief from the ongoing thoughts playing on repeat in your head? Thoughts that make you relive hard and even hurtful situations over and over again. Sometimes the tendency is to ignore them and pray the darkness suffocates or shrinks them into non-existence.

During some alone time with God, I decided to let Him hear all the thoughts I had been dwelling on and all the situations I knew I couldn't change. Knowing this fact didn't stop them from lilting to and fro in my head like a ship in the midst of the high seas.

I have been trying to navigate these high seas by not complaining. I went to the opposite extreme and just left it there, unattended.

Do you remember cleaning out the fridge that had science experiments growing inside of it, because of ignoring the food that was hidden in the dark? When situations are left in the dark and ignored sometimes, the darkness has the potential to make it grow into something more powerful than we anticipated. It started happening to me. I didn't like the way it made me feel. As a result, I decided to bring it all out into the light where it could be fed the truth, grow something good in me, and weed out the roots of darkness.

After I finished telling God every single burden, I decided to "be still" and listen. He never disappoints when we decide to trust Him with everything. He will always show up when we choose to drag things into the light instead of stuffing them in the shadows.

He heard my cries. He acknowledged my heartache!
No fireworks!
No lightning strikes!
Only sweet peace!

He didn't point fingers and He didn't do any condemning. He gave me three important truths to consider as I make my way through hard situations.

First Truth: I do not get a free pass from doing right because a situation I encountered wounded me. My heart has to remain focused on the eternal.

Second Truth: The battle for my heart is ongoing. I haven't arrived and I have to continue to be intentional and keep fighting in the light.

Third Truth: "Dwell in My love."
Bask in the light of the last truth and all the other situations will be turned into lanterns lighting your way on the path He has put before you.

Dear Lord, Help us to dwell in Your love through every circumstance. Help us to realize the heartache we face and the situations we encounter are "not against flesh and blood, but against the spiritual forces in the heavenly realm." Lord, We will praise You because you are our true North in the midst of every high sea! Amen

My thoughts:

_____

_____

_____

_____

_____

_____

△ △ △

AMAZING LOVE
by Lori Reynolds Streller

"He was delivered over to death for our sins and was raised to life for our justification." Romans 4:25 NIV

I sit in a doctor's waiting room again today; walking the cold, sterile halls to an exam room; discussing symptoms and pain issues with a specialist. This time I am with my daughter instead of my husband, but the memories flood me just the same.

No, she doesn't have cancer. No, her condition isn't life threatening. But the hours spent with her through an exam and then in the lab for massive blood draws were all too familiar to me.

She has some type of autoimmune disease, one that is hard to pinpoint and diagnose; a chronic illness that doesn't present with typical symptoms. The fact that her disease is unknown doesn't eliminate the reality of her joint pain. It doesn't dismiss that she has sat out of Cross Country and Softball seasons because it hurts too much to do the things she enjoys.

I don't like seeing my daughter suffer.

No parent likes to see their child suffering.
Ahhhhh, and with that thought, the light bulb blinks on in my heart.

NO PARENT...

God the Father did not enjoy seeing His Son suffering.

In Matthew 26:38–39 Jesus Christ was overwhelmed with sorrow. He asked God to take the cup of suffering from Him.

Can you even imagine? The all-powerful God, who could end the suffering of His Son, chose not to. I cannot comprehend the restraint that must have taken. What intense heartache.

Jesus finishes His request with these nine words, *"Yet not as I will, but as You will."*

Oh how the Father must have been beaming with pride over his Son's submission; a total submission that led all the way to the cross.

Christ asked again in verse 42, *"My Father, if it is not possible for this cup to be taken away unless I drink it, may Your will be done."*

And again, in verse 44 Jesus makes His same request. This repeated plea for help coupled with unwavering willingness to obey shakes me to my core.

I want to stop the pain my daughter experiences on a daily basis. I cannot.

God's love for us is so unfathomably great, that He allowed His Son to suffer, knowing it was the only way for us to spend eternity with Him. Even knowing that Christ would be victorious over death, God's heart must have grieved at His suffering. Jesus's cup of suffering was the separation from God that would occur when He took on the sins of the world. He faced a double death. I imagine that spiritual separation was even more painful than the physical death for Christ.

Jesus, being God Himself, was given the power to lay down His life. (John 10:17-18) He, as the Son of God, always obeys the will of His Father. He stayed on the cross. He stayed to become our way of salvation.

God didn't stop Jesus' suffering.

He is God the Father. He knows what it is like to watch a child suffer and yet His love for us is so vast that He permitted it.

I wouldn't choose for my child to suffer in order for me to have a relationship with you, sister. I certainly wouldn't expect you to sacrifice your child in order to know me. Yet that's exactly what God did for each of us.

He
amazes
me.

Thank You, Lord, that You are a loving God. Your love for us transcends our knowledge. Watching my child suffer the slightest bit grieves my heart. I cannot wrap my brain around the depth of Your love for mankind that You would sacrifice Your Son for our redemption, but I am so grateful that You did. You amaze me, Lord. Amen.

My thoughts:

_____

_____

_____

_____

_____

_____

_____

_____

_____

_____

_____

_____

_____

_____

_____

_____

_____

_____

_____

△ △ △

DEARLY LOVED
by Sheryl Pepple

Therefore, as God's chosen people, holy and dearly loved, clothe yourselves with compassion, kindness, humility, gentleness and patience. Bear with each other and forgive whatever grievances you may have against one another. Forgive as the Lord forgave you. And over all these virtues put on love, which binds them all together in perfect unity.

Colossians 3:12 ESV

His word is His love letter to us. Sometimes we are in so much pain it is hard to remember that He is there. He is. Take some time today to spend with Him, pour out your heart to Him. He will answer. Below is a copy of my first letter to God since my husband's death on September 12, 2011, it was written just thirteen days after his death. I poured out my heart to God, and He was there. On that day and many days since, He has reminded me that I am holy and dearly loved.

Dear Heavenly Father,
I sit before you today as your child with a broken heart...but all the pieces are yours. As much as I love my husband, miss him and struggle with this unbearable pain– I love you more than anything or

anyone. You gave me that gift, a heart that loves you through all things. As much as my mind struggles with the losses I have experienced–I love you more. As much as I struggle with wanting to be brought home and delivered from this world, this pain, I love you more. Your word tells me in Col 3:12 that as God's chosen people (which I am) I am holy and dearly loved. Lord, I am struggling with this pain but I know two things: 1) you are sovereign over everything and everyone and 2) you are good. I thank you for that wisdom and the strength that comes from your truth. I feel broken and of no value but I know that you live in me and that you will continue to fulfill your purposes through me. My life is not my own, it is yours. It was bought for a price and now through my husband's death I have a better appreciation of the price that was paid. Lord, there is so much I don't understand but I do know your will is perfect, pleasing and acceptable. I know that I am not to lean on my own understanding. Lord, I hurt, I am broken, but I am your chosen one, I am holy and dearly loved.

I pray that today you will pour out your heart to God and let Him comfort you as only He can. I pray that you will be reminded that you are Holy and Dearly Loved!

If you are uncertain if you are His chosen one, then cry out to Him and ask Him to be Lord of your life. He will answer.

John 3:16
For God so loved the world that he gave his one and only Son, that whoever believes in him shall not perish but have eternal life.

My thoughts:

_____

_____

_____

_____

_____

_____

_____

_____

_____

_____

_____

△ △ △

LOVE SO DEEP
by Leah Stirewalt

Within one week of my husband's death, I returned to blogging again. Some might find that rather strange and untimely. For me...very therapeutic. As a lover of words, yet unable to form many with my mouth during those early weeks, I turned to my other passion...writing. I kept a journal (and still do) but find most of my thoughts then (and now) get poured out on my personal blog site.

Shockingly, a new world opened up for me, one that I was completely oblivious to before my husband's suicide. I began receiving blog comments, email messages, Facebook comments, and even Twitter love – mostly aimed at encouraging me through the darkest days I'd ever experienced in my thirty-nine years. Even more, I became acquainted with strangers – many of whom I now call friends – that are also widows themselves (some even by suicide). I began to realize I wasn't alone. I knew I wasn't the only one that had walked the same road. But, I also knew I needed some help and certainly couldn't do this alone.

This grief journey is not for the faint at heart. The tough, independent woman of yesteryear no longer seemed to be around. I found myself quite needy actually – a word I never associated myself with before. I went through the motions of living each day, but I couldn't accomplish much more than that. Decision making? Virtually impossible. Food prep? Forget about it. House cleaning? I couldn't care less.

Nevertheless, I was blessed with an army of helpmates to fill in the gaps. Friends from church, co-workers, neighbors, family, and even complete strangers became my angels of mercy. God poured out His comfort on us in amazing ways through His children. I will never forget that tremendous blessing in those early weeks.

A month passed. Life started to become "real" again.

Deep loneliness set in. I found myself seeking that "help" again. Anyone out there? I couldn't expect people to continue to lavish personal attention upon us forever, but I wasn't ready for it to end so abruptly. In all actuality, it didn't end. We're still being cared for (8 months later) in some rather amazing ways, but the huge saturation of daily care did stop. And, I really understood that. People have lives to live outside of serving new Widow Leah and her daughter. I just wasn't ready for it.

It was then God's voice became quite loud to me. He wanted to be the center of my need. And, in the stillness of our times together, He spoke frequently to my heart.

Am I enough daughter?
If I take it all away...will you still return to Me?
Can you trust Me to care for you completely?
Do you know how massive My love is for you?

"Yes Lord! Of course! You are enough. I'll always return to You. Of course I trust You, and I know You love me deeply."

But, He wouldn't stop. I don't think He was satisfied with my answer. Maybe because it was what I thought He wanted to hear.

I know your heart, Leah. Remember, I crafted it. You can hide nothing from Me.

Again, am I enough? Will you always return to Me? Can you completely trust Me? Do you know the depth of My love?

"OK, Father. You want the truth. Here it goes...
I say You're enough, but I haven't lost all yet. Chris wasn't my everything, but he was pretty close. I say I'll always return to You. Lord, I pray that to always be true. I can't imagine life without You. But, if I don't stay near to You, I'm sure even I can develop a wandering heart. Please protect me from ever wandering from You sweet Lord!

As for trusting...I need You to really help me with this one. I have nobody to fully trust but You, but I'm struggling here, Lord. How's that for honesty? You're the only One I can always trust and yet I'm struggling to do just that. What's wrong with me?"

I can tell you what's wrong, my beloved daughter. You don't understand the depth of My love for you. And, you never fully understand it completely this side of paradise, but allow Me to show you as much as you will open your physical eyes to see. Even more of My love will be shown to you through your eyes of faith. And one day daughter...one blessed day...your faith will become your sight! Until that day, rest Leah...rest in Me! I want to carry all of your pain, because I love you completely!

My thoughts:

_____

_____

_____

_____

_____

_____

_____

_____

_____

_____

_____

_____

_____

_____

_____

△ △ △

THE CURTAIN IS TORN
by Sheryl Pepple

And when Jesus had cried out again in a loud voice, he gave up his spirit.
At that moment, the curtain of the temple was torn in two from top to bottom. The earth shook and the rocks split. The tombs broke open and the bodies of many holy people who had died were raised to life.

Matthew 27:50-53 (NIV)

I must confess... some days I want to give up.

It is hard to miss my husband so much every day, but particularly around the holidays. Those special days will never quite be the joyous celebration they used to be. We were so caught up in the hustle and bustle of the holidays, temporarily forgetting our troubles and worries as we rushed around with parties and gift buying. It was so much fun to start a New Year, dream about what was to come and plan the vacations we would take. It was as if we had separated ourselves from the world and anything bad by putting up a curtain.

And then, in the blink of an eye, my husband was gone, killed by a drunk driver. The "curtain" was torn forever. It is no longer possible to forget the bad things. I live every day with the knowledge that death can intrude in an instant. I live with the pain of missing my husband and the way our life once was. The curtain has been torn – things will never be the same.

Thankfully, I am reminded of another curtain that has been torn – the one at the temple. It was torn the moment Jesus gave up His spirit on the Cross. Prior to that moment, the curtain at the temple separated us from the Most Holy. And then, because of God's grace, it was torn, from the top to the bottom, reconciling us with Him, once and forever.

Because of that torn curtain, we are never alone. God is with us! He is with us on those days we can't get out of bed. He is with us when we look at that empty chair at the table. He is with us when those tears come –yet again. He loves us so much, He allowed His Son to die on the Cross. How precious are we that He would pay such a price. We cannot take the pain of the death of a loved one lightly. We know only too well the cost. Because of the torn curtain, I know without a doubt, He loves me. It changes everything.

I have to let that soak in, again and again – He loves me. He created me. Nothing I can do will ever change His love for me. He cares about each tear I shed. He cares about each step I take. He has a purpose for my life -even now - when I feel so broken. Maybe it is especially now – when I am so broken.

As I continue healing, I see the curtain we put up to separate us from suffering can also separate us from God. Because it is in our suffering, we cry out to Him, walk with Him, and eventually become more like Him.

Dear Sisters, celebrate today that the curtain has been torn. It changes everything. Don't give up. He loves you. Walk with Him!

My thoughts:

_____

_____

_____

_____

_____

_____

_____

△ △ △

MY BEST FRIEND
by Karen Emberlin

There is a friend who sticks closer than a brother...Proverbs 18:24 (NIV)

Yes, my husband "was" my best friend! Together, we shared hopes for the future, dreams that never came true, goals that were never achieved, and the many disappointments life sent our way.

However, we also shared many wonderful experiences together. When they happened, he was always the first person I wanted to tell, because I knew he would share in my excitement.

When I was sad, he was always there to cheer me up. I knew his shoulder was there to cry on, and he gave the best hugs in the world! He made me feel very special and beautiful, and every morning he would tell me I was his "angel." I knew he truly loved me and cared about me.

I could tell him things that I've never shared with another soul. He absorbed everything I said, and actually wanted to hear more. Many times there was no need for continuous conversation, I was quite content in just having him nearby. He also seemed to know what I was thinking, even without asking me!

Things that never interested me before became fascinating because I knew they were important to him, and he was so special to me.

Nearly fifty years ago, I opened my heart to him and experienced a love and friendship I never dreamed was possible. My husband was my best friend and much more ... until his last breath.

Life is completely different now without my husband as my best friend! Simple things still bring him to my mind every day. Even though time keeps moving on, I miss him more than ever, and oh, how I would like to be able to talk with him and hear his voice again, or just sit in his presence! I know there will never be another person on this earth who will be the friend to me that my husband was. In spite of all these "feelings," I know God's plan was to take my husband home, and I am very thankful for every day I was able to spend with him.

As a child, I opened my heart to Jesus as my Savior. As I continue this journey of widowhood, my love for Him keeps growing and I am becoming more dependent on Him each day. I am beginning to realize He is a friend who is even more significant in my life than my husband was.

As I look over the things my husband and I enjoyed as friends, I find that Jesus is there to fulfill all of those things, plus more!

Look at just a few examples with me:
- He has plans for my future – Jeremiah 29:11
- I am the apple of His eye – Psalm 17:8
- He gives me peace of mind – John 16:33
- He loves me and is holding my right hand – Psalm 73:23
- He knows when I am upset and collects my tears in a bottle – Psalm 56:8
- He supplies all my needs – Philippians 4:19
- He will listen to me and will answer me– I John 5:14-15
- He takes me in His arms – Mark 10:16
- He strengthens me – Philippians 4:13

Oh, What A Friend We Have In Jesus! But, how much peace do we forfeit and how much needless pain do we bear, all because we do not carry everything to God in prayer! (from the hymn by Joseph Scriven, What a Friend We Have in Jesus)

Lord, You know how much I miss my husband and the friendship we had together. Let me never forget the friendship and peace I can have when I bring everything to You. Thank You for being the best Friend I could ever want! Amen.

My thoughts:

_____

_____

_____

_____

_____

_____

_____

_____

_____

_____

_____

_____

△ △ △

Section 3: Healing Begins with Hope

Psalm 121:1-8 NIV

I lift up my eyes to the mountains—
where does my help come from?
My help comes from the Lord,
the Maker of heaven and earth.
He will not let your foot slip—
he who watches over you will not slumber;
Indeed, he who watches over Israel
will neither slumber nor sleep.
The Lord watches over you—
the Lord is your shade at your right hand;
the sun will not harm you by day,
nor the moon by night.
The Lord will keep you from all harm—
he will watch over your life;
the Lord will watch over your coming and going
both now and forevermore.

5 THINGS TO HELP YOU HEAL
by Elizabeth Dyer Colvard

Everywhere I look I see articles on 5 things. Sometimes these are called "click bait" because they just want you to click on them to get you to their websites. I get so interested in article after article on childhood stars (where are they now?) or bad foods (what to avoid to lose 20 lbs by tomorrow) and so on.

I found 5 things you and I can start doing today, to lead to a happier, healthier, and more healed life. They are just as relevant today as they were when they were written thousands of years ago.

Have I got your attention?

Here they are.

Psalm 119:13-16 NIV
With my lips I recount all the laws that come from your mouth.
I rejoice in following your statutes as one rejoices in great riches.
I meditate on your precepts and consider your ways.

I delight in your decrees; I will not neglect your word.

One of my first pieces of advice I give when someone is going through hard circumstances is to read the Psalms. To me, they seem like peeking into a journal of an old time Bible character-his personal blog before blogging! The authors get mad, they get sad, they complain, they rejoice--sometimes all in the same chapter! Doesn't that sound a little familiar?

But the Psalms have a way of focusing my attention and regaining perspective.

Recount. Start with journaling how God has taken care of you in the past. How God has walked beside you. How God has sent others to hold your arms up in the battle. How Scripture or songs have come on at just the right time you needed them.

Rejoice. Rejoice as one who has won the lottery. I have never even bought a lottery ticket so for me to win would be some major big-time rejoicing! The rejoicing in this verse is pointing at following God's laws. We might interpret it as rejoicing in living according to Scripture.

Meditate. Give thought throughout the day. We can only do that when we are focused on Scripture as we START the day. I have to work at this still. I can easily get distracted by my life, social media, or the news. It seems like an inconvenience sometimes to take the time to read, but it is always a blessing when I do. I am trying to read through the entire Bible. It has taken me a year and a half to get halfway through; but it sure helps me meditate on eternal things.

Delight. Like in a scrumptious dessert. Look forward to spending time in Scripture. Look forward to spending time in worship with other believers. Sing along with the praise songs on the radio.

I will NOT neglect your word. I've already confessed that spending time in God's Word is still something I have to remind myself to do. I miss days too often. Then, I always have a lame excuse for why I skipped my time in the Word. It can be easy in our early grief to neglect the Scripture because it is too hard to get our brains to focus. But, I believe the Holy Spirit will help us when we ask for focus. God WANTS us to spend time in His Word.

The Psalmist gives us some things we can start doing today. Which one can you add to your life?

~ Recount
~ Rejoice
~ Meditate
~ Delight
~ Not neglect God's Word.

Do these 5 things every day and you will be happier. I guarantee it.
Or your money back. ;)

Lord, You want me in Your Word. Give me focus today to dig into Scripture. Help me recount the ways You have protected me or answered prayers in the past. I want to follow Your Word today. Amen

My thoughts:

_____

_____

_____

_____

_____

△ △ △

HALF TO WHOLE AGAIN
by Jennifer Stanton Boswell

January 15, 2015.
Half of me was severed that day.
Abruptly gone.

As I think back to that day and those first moments, my heart still begins to race. My hands start to sweat and my stomach is filled with an uneasiness that cannot be described.

That day ... that day I was forever changed.

It's been three years since our world shattered and my hopes and dreams for our lives were immediately taken. I knew there was no earthly way I was strong enough or brave enough to continue life without my husband Michael. And, I was right. No "earthly way" could save me, only the Lord.

Night after night, I called out to Him, "Jesus, help me." And, He did. The Lord placed people in my life who surrounded me with love and support, and I leaned into them, hard. He gave me the courage to seek help through counseling, and I opened up about my loss and how I felt like never before.

The Lord's strength helped me fight for my life - His strength put my feet on the floor every morning so I could be the mom I needed to be for my son. His strength brought me out of the darkness. His strength lifted me from the ashes. He has brought restoration, hope and happiness into my life after loss of such magnitude. He wants to do this for you, too.

As widows, when we lose our husbands – it's true – half is gone, but there is hope in being whole again through Jesus. We can be complete in Christ if we lean into Him. He promises this.

And in Christ you have been brought to fullness. He is the head over every power and authority. Colossians 2:10 (NIV)

Being confident of this, that he who began a good work in you will carry it on to completion until the day of Christ. Philippians 1:6 (NIV)

That's good news, sisters: For those of us who are believers, we are complete in Him! The Lord wants all of His children to call on Him. So let us not focus on our weaknesses and what we lack on this earth, but instead focus on the Lord's strength, wholeness and completeness that is already in US.

Lord, I pray for each of my sisters, that they may find wholeness in You. It can be easy to focus on what we lack, but remind us that YOU are all we need. Thank You for Your faithfulness. Amen.

My thoughts:

_____

_____

_____

_____

_____

_____

_____

_____

_____

_____

_____

_____

△ △ △

HANGING ON TO HOPE
by Elizabeth Dyer Colvard

What are you hoping for right now?

Hoping that your car can keep limping along?

Maybe you're hoping for a better job to come along soon.

Perhaps some are hoping to get married again.

Are you just hoping the money can hold out?

As widows, our hopes probably run the gamut. Every time I am at the craft and hobby store I see cute signs to hang on the wall that say HOPE. Just plain hope. Are we supposed to hang onto some vague concept of hope?

Some days, like today, I have not felt hopeful. I don't see how we will ever be financially 'comfortable' again. I don't hope anymore for the 'white horse rescue'. That word HOPE kept showing up places all this week. On social media. In stores. In songs. Frankly, I have grown tired of it. I want to shout, It doesn't mean what you think it means! But I restrained myself. Sometimes I struggle even knowing what it means!

So what should I hope?

As I kept pondering the word, I looked for Scripture to show me what we should be hoping. Here's what I found. I hope it helps you focus on what our hope should be.

H: Heaven -- the hope laid up for you in heaven. Colossians 1:5 I find myself wishing for heaven but not always for the "right" reasons. Do you find yourself hoping for heaven because your late husband is there? Heaven is far more than that.

O: Overcome -- In the world you will have tribulation. But take heart; I have overcome the world. John 16:33 It gives me immense hope when I remind myself that Christ has conquered the sorrows and difficulties of the fallen world. Why am I so surprised when the trials and tribulations come my way? I WILL have them. But I can have HOPE in the rough times because this life isn't all there is.

P: Peace-- May the God of hope fill you with all joy and peace in believing, so that by the power of the Holy Spirit you may abound in hope. Romans 15:13 What is the opposite of peace? I think of chaos. How can we have a supernatural calmness when our circumstances seem full of chaos? I believe it has to do with focus once again. Our hearts can be so connected with Christ that His hope and joy fills us through the Holy Spirit. It can't be explained any other way. It is like an invisible power cord from our hearts to heaven!

E: Eternal Comfort -- Now may our Lord Jesus Christ himself, and God our Father, who loved us and gave us eternal comfort and good hope through grace, comfort your hearts and establish them in every good work and word. 2 Thessalonians 2:16-17 It appears that every verse I found proves this hope is from God - and this verse says He GAVE us this comfort and hope. Money and sex cannot promise you the comfort you crave. Only Christ. That void you feel in your soul can only be satisfied through your Creator.

*all scripture from ESV

I'm going to recall these words of H.O.P.E. when my heart feels hopeless. Because over and over, I have found that my feelings cannot be trusted.

Hope is found in Christ.

Let that sink deep into your souls today, friend.

Father God, Your Word gives us encouragement and hope. Forgive us for filling our hearts with other things that never satisfy. We want to be more diligent in digging into Your Word on a daily basis. Amen

My thoughts:

_____

_____

_____

_____

_____

_____

_____

△ △ △

I HAVE CALMED AND QUIETED MY SOUL
by Terri Oxner Sharp

Calm and quiet never felt so far away!

"This can't be real!
It wasn't supposed to be this way!
Please let me wake up from this nightmare!"

These phrases were just a few of the deafening screams
of my broken heart in the early days of my grief.
`

The trauma surrounding the sudden death of my
husband brought with it an inner turmoil I had never
experienced before.

Four words from a police officer changed my life
forever.

"We couldn't save him."

Those words echoed in my mind, day and night.

Suddenly, decisions and arrangements had to be made
at a time when I had little energy or coherent thought

to make them. My children needed me; that is all I could concentrate on for very long.

Helplessly torn between my own need to grieve and the responsibilities of being there for my children, my inner struggle was to remain calm. I certainly did not feel calm! For the first time I really understood the "fight or flight" response I read about in textbooks.

I wanted to leave; to be anywhere I could grieve without hurting someone else.

While I was determined to be real with people about the anguish I felt, I never wanted to burden others with my grief.

My world had just collapsed. How was I supposed to go on?

Then God reminded me through His Word,
Peace I leave with you, My peace I give to you. Not as the world gives do I give to you. Let not your hearts be troubled, neither let them be afraid. John 14:27 (ESV)

As a believer, I had the promise of the everlasting peace of Christ!

This was a comfort to my weary soul. Yet knowing the promise and repeating it to myself did not always keep fear at bay.

Precious friends and family members were incredibly supportive, but I knew at the end of each day, grief in its chaos was waiting for me to continue down the pathway alone. Overall, it is not a pathway wide enough for two.

I knew I was not strong enough to walk it alone.

Once again, God gently reminded me through His Word.

I was NOT alone! The path was narrow and dark but He would carry me! Though the comfort of humans was temporary and never enough, God's comfort would continue and was ultimately all I needed.

Psalm 131:1-3 (ESV) says,
O Lord, my heart is not lifted up; my eyes are not raised too high; I do not occupy myself with things too great and too marvelous for me. But I have calmed and quieted my soul, like a weaned child with its mother; like a weaned child is

my soul within me. O Israel, hope in the Lord from this time forth and forevermore.

Like Israel, my hope was and is in the Lord!

Though I had nothing, in and of myself, that would calm or quiet my soul, I had faith in the One I trust with my future.

God has faithfully carried me along my grief journey, through every dark twist and turn in my path, and into the light of joy on the other side. He has never failed to be there.

His promise of peace is real, His footing on the path is sure, and His presence brings a calm and quiet for the soul who abides in Him.

Experience peace, calm, quiet, and yes, even joy! Abide in Him!

Father, please help us to abide in You. Let us cling to Your promise of a peace that You do not remove once You give it to us. You tell us not to be troubled or afraid; with You guiding us we have nothing to fear. There is nothing about our circumstances that catches You by surprise. We can trust

You to carry us through the times when our minds cannot comprehend how to continue living without our loved ones. Help us to calm and quiet our souls like David did, by meditating on the Truth of Your Word. Amen

My thoughts:

_____

_____

_____

_____

_____

_____

_____

_____

_____

_____

_____

△ △ △

A CALLING FOR COMMUNITY
by Katie Hagen

What if you don't have to do this alone?

What if we weren't meant to live in these bubbles of self-sufficiency ready to pop with priorities we manage and overflowing daily planners? What if God's given us assistants?

I've trained myself to put one foot in front of the other and run on adrenaline. Tell this lady to 'just do her best and forget the rest' and I'll offer a sincere smile, nodding yet dismissing the wisdom in your words.

Why?

I've learned to define success as self-sufficiency and independence. Asking for help means I'm not working hard enough or measuring up high enough.

HELP: A four letter word in my personal pocket dictionary defined as 'weakness'. Truth is, I innocently just want to make my own way under the radar not coming across as a nuisance or inadequate.

So, me ask for help? Not even when widowhood wears me so thin I can hardly withstand the wind. Not when single motherhood has my knees hitting the floor in frustration.

But this stops me short: Ecclesiastes 4: 9–12. I'd glossed over it before but the timing wasn't right. Now it hits me square in the stubborn, seemingly self-sufficient head.

"Two are better than one, because they have a better return for their work: If one falls down, his friend can help him up. But pity the man who falls and has not one to help pick him up! Also if two lie down together, they will keep warm. But how can one keep warm alone? Though one may be overpowered, two can defend themselves. A chord of three strands is not quickly broken."

Lord, I just want to serve You! But, maybe servant-hood doesn't mean living without need in my own life....

I've been sacrificing self-care.... no, 'soul care', to live in self-sufficiency. The stress of trying to do it all alone deters me from God's plan for me.

Standing alone on an unknowing pedestal of perfectionism, sacrificing soul-care, until I'm shivering in the cold. Ouch!

But, me? Risk vulnerability in need of help?

Read again those Biblical words. Are you convicted like I or comforted by the sense of community?

I long for the former, a life alongside Christian comrades supporting each other in community. So, I'm aiming to soften my solitary ways.

I'm calling out more often, learning to accept assistance. When I'm simply worn thin not needing a hand, there's warmth just in knowing someone's there to pick me up, encourage me, to offer perspective or validation.

God says we were made for companionship...Christian companionship. I've often avoided the idea because it reminds me of the love I lost when my husband left for heaven. But I'm certain romantic love isn't what God meant here: 'A cord of three strands is not quickly broken.'

He wants us to work together, hold up, hold on to and defend each other. Who am I to go against that Godly grain?!

Community. Companionship. It comes at a cost but there's such value in vulnerability!

Jesus formed churches to gather in worship, God gave us governments to guide and created cultures to thrive...all communities with common goals. Each time we lean into a Christian community we feel a sense of inclusion.

But it's not only inclusion we need. As women and moms working hard we require validation, too.

Why not tip toe off our pedestals to faithfully fill our needs through the hands of helpers God gave us? Rather than a nuisance, it offers others opportunity to obey God's command to serve one another.

Our turn will arrive to open hearts and lend the loving hand.

Through community we are held up and held accountable. We give and receive, support and seek.

I now know I wasn't made to do 'life' alone. I value the village God built around my little family.

I use my time and talents but without tapping myself out. When I white knuckle the wheel of over-commitment I easily fall further from God, even when I'm giving!

Do you feel it too? In the stress of doing everything alone do you become distracted from the life He wants you to live, losing touch with what's important?

Take it from a former overly independent martyr (I mean mother!): Stay close to a Christian community. Spiritually, occupationally and even at home, you're not alone.

Let's go forth together and build a world of encouragers, of Lord lovers and of Christians in community. Let's live this blessed life together supporting each other and praising our Savior...let's live in community because, after all, we've already got enough critics!

My thoughts:

_____

_____

_____

_____

_____

_____

_____

_____

_____

_____

_____

_____

_____

_____

_____

_____

_____

_____

_____

_____

_____

△ △ △

FOUR STRONG CORNERS
by Linda Lint

Man shall not live and be upheld and sustained by bread alone, but by every word that comes forth from the mouth of God. Matthew 4:4 (Amplified Version)

When we married, I brought with me the delight of assembling jigsaw puzzles. It quickly became a hobby we enjoyed together. We could spend hours, and sometimes days, putting together a large, complicated puzzle. We had a routine – first sorting through all the pieces to find the edges and corners, then proceed to fit together the remaining pieces based on that framework – and having the reference picture on the box helped a lot!

Occasionally, we would get side-tracked and attempt to assemble the puzzle without the frame being in place. We found this was never really successful and led to frustration and wasted time. He made frames for them and they still hang throughout our home. I treasure them.

Every once in a while, we would end up with a piece missing after the puzzle was completed. Sometimes, it was a body piece. Sometimes it was an edge or even a corner piece. It seemed we could overlook the missing body piece but the absence of that edge or corner piece was very apparent and the puzzle was useless for framing.

I still love to assemble puzzles. However, due to space limits and a very "helpful" cat, I now assemble the puzzles online. The process is the same, however. First, the corners and edges – then the rest. Occasionally the site offers a "challenge" puzzle to assemble with just a title – no reference picture. It is pointless for me to attempt assembly without the corner and edge pieces in place. The puzzle frame is the only reference I have to continue.

While I was working on the most recent challenge, I was thinking about how my life now is similar to the "challenge" puzzle experience.

I have in front of me a large group of puzzle pieces. I have a title "Linda's life now without her husband". I must work on getting this puzzle together. It is the corner and edge pieces that will give me a strong start – a solid foundation in putting this picture together.

My four strong corners come straight from God's Word: (New Living Translation)

- When I have trouble sleeping: *Psalm 4:8 "In peace I will lie down and sleep. For You alone Lord God cause me to dwell in safety."*
- When storms blow in: *Proverbs 15:25 "The Lord tears down the house of the proud, but He protects the property of widows."*
- When I am concerned about repairmen and business dealings: *Deuteronomy 10:18 "He ensures that orphans and widows receive justice."*
- When I miss my husband and need to talk: *Isaiah 54:5 "For your Creator will be your husband; the Lord of Heaven's Armies is His name. He is your redeemer, the Holy One of Israel, the God of all the earth."*

These four strong corners anchor the framework of my life now - and a truly solid anchor it is. It will take the remainder of my days to complete this particular "challenge" puzzle. But, that's ok - because the corners and edges are solid and I have the promise of God's Word that when the last piece is in place I will be joining Him in Heaven!

Father: Your Word is our life. It sustains us and gives us strength. We know we can rely on it totally to guide us through this life-time assembly process. We are so very grateful. Amen

My thoughts:

_____

_____

_____

_____

_____

_____

_____

_____

_____

_____

_____

_____

_____

△ △ △

I DON'T HAVE TO BE TOUGH
by Ami Atkins Wickiser

...showing honor to the woman as the weaker vessel, since they are heirs with you of the grace of life... I Peter 3:7 ESV

I got up early, showered, straightened my hair, and overall just looked cute. I thought about corporate worship, and couldn't wait to be with the church. What snow? I'd be just fine.

Opening my garage door, I wasn't surprised to see several inches of the white stuff and more still falling. "No problem. I've got this."

I backed out slowly. All was well; there was no getting stuck in this driveway.

Well, until I got stuck, that is.

The wheels spun, and the engine revved. But it was just a show. Hmm, that was futile.

First action step, call a friend, of course. A true gentleman, he offered to come get me. Meekly, I accepted.

In the meantime, I shoveled with determination and perhaps stubbornness. At least I could get it back in the garage, right?

I'll spare you all the grisly details, but I ended up wet, covered in snow, mad, crying, and no closer to getting the car unstuck. The wind was unforgiving, hurling snow at places I'd already cleared. And you can forget that lovely, straightened hair.

Tears stung my face. I was angry that I no longer had a husband to take care of such things. I was angry that I couldn't do it, and angry I had to ask for help. When I called my friend back, I felt like an incapable wimp. "Don't come get me."

"Why?"

"I'm so angry and upset that I can't get my car out. I'm mad that I have to, and not at all in the right place to be at church."

"Ami, you're being ridiculous. I'm coming to get you," my guy friend calmly replied.

Later during worship, he slipped me a note. "I need your car keys. Several of us are going to go over and get you unstuck."

Tears formed again, yet these were full of gratitude. I'm strong in many ways, but it's okay to admit my weaknesses.

I am weaker in physical strength than men, but that's not a bad thing.

So, here are the lessons.

Culture says, "Be a strong, tough, independent woman." But God honors women as the "weaker vessel." I don't mean that women aren't capable, but our Lord says be honored, cherished, protected. Be the fine china. My pastor put it this way, "A chivalrous man takes the bullets, does the nasty work, and gets dirty because he realizes a lady shouldn't have to."

> *...showing honor to the woman as the weaker vessel.*
> *I Peter 3:7 ESV*

"Weaker vessel" doesn't mean it's inferior or any less valued. Rather, it is to be protected, esteemed, more highly valued.

That's a difficult thing for widows to hear. "Who's protecting me now? Who is doing the nasty work? Quite frankly, I have to do it a lot these days, " my heart cries.

Yes, that's often true, but it's okay to ask for help. Sometimes it's even needed. I know that's a challenge, but people may not know the need until we ask. While Peter is speaking specifically to husbands in the verse above, there's broader application within the church. Men can still honor the women around them with appropriate boundaries.

Being cared for is a lovely thing. I miss my chivalrous husband dearly, but I'm thankful God still puts chivalrous men in my life- family, friends, pastors. I'm thankful for men who help with home repairs, lift heavy objects, and pick me up in a blizzard.

I don't have to be tough.

Father, ultimately You are the One who protects and provides. But it's difficult to be on my own. Give me grace to seek help when I need it, and grace to accept help when I need it. Please provide for my fellow sisters, that they may be cherished and valued. Amen.

My thoughts:

_____

_____

_____

_____

_____

_____

_____

_____

_____

_____

_____

_____

_____

_____

_____

_____

_____

△ △ △

HAVE YOU HEARD?
by Erika Graham

O magnify the LORD with me, And let us exalt His name together.

Psalms 34:3 (NASB)

Have you heard?
"I am a widow."

Yep, for different reasons, I've said that a great deal this week. It's a phrase I have grown accustomed to, even though I still don't like it all the time.

Widowhood is a badge to me--a badge I wear every day. Whether I speak the words or not, it's with me. Like a wheelchair to a person who can't walk, or a shiny medal on a uniform, or even the spattered food and wrappers strewn about my car from my kids. Each of these is a symbol of identity. And widowhood is one of the badges that is a part of my identity.

Some days that badge looks amazing and is displayed proudly. It is an honor to be Scott's widow. It is an honor to have been loved well and to have loved well. It's an honor to have married my childhood sweetheart, my best friend. It's an honor to have those precious few years where we started a life together, built a home, and brought three precious babies into this world. It's an honor God has allowed me to heal and grow, that He has "chosen" me to walk this journey. That He has set me apart, and is equipping me to do all He has in store for me.

On the good days, that's how this looks and sounds.
But sometimes, my widow badge is tarnished, nasty, and gnarly looking and I just want to cover it up and hide it. It's so painful and sad to talk about my love. When I have to verbalize the overwhelming loss I feel on a daily basis, or even identify my lot to someone, it stings badly. When the grief wells up on holidays, anniversaries, and other not-so-significant days, it makes me want to pretend like it doesn't exist. And when my kids cry out for their dad, when they long for him, and their pain and sadness engulfs them, that's when I want to just blight it out.

I don't talk about being a widow every day. But, every day, widowhood is a part of me and is my "badge of honor," whether I am verbalizing it to someone or not. It's an honor because I had the privilege of being in a wonderful marriage and I experienced becoming a mom with my best friend three times over. And yes, no matter how much I don't like it, it's an honor God is using my loss for His glory, that He is allowing me to find such purpose in my suffering. He has given me the opportunity to be comforted, so I can then comfort others.

Most importantly, it's a great honor that I can honor God throughout!

Father God, thank You for allowing me to be a wife, so I can now be a widow. No matter how hard it is or how much I want to hide it some days, help me to see Your greater purposes. Heal me, Lord, and continue to help me bring all honor and glory to You as I have opportunities to share my story to those in my world. Help me share boldly, no matter the response or awkwardness. In Your Matchless Name, Amen.

My thoughts:

△ △ △

Section 4: Being in Community

Though one may be overpowered,
two can defend themselves.
A cord of three strands
is not quickly broken.

Ecclesiastes 4:13 NIV

ISOLATION IS THE ENEMY
by Jennifer Stanton Boswell

All alone. Isolated.

That's what this journey can feel like, especially those first hours, days, weeks and months – just trying to survive. Losing our husbands, it can be easy to step away from it all, retreat and isolate ourselves and dwell on our circumstances. After all, that is what seems natural when our world falls apart.

Over the past couple of weeks, the pastor at my church has discussed the topic of isolation in our everyday lives, which got me thinking ... if everyday circumstances cause us to isolate, becoming a widow is more than enough reason. But this is exactly the opposite of what God wants for us.

- *For the body does not consist of one member but of many. 1 Corinthians 12:14 (ESV)*

- *Whoever isolates himself seeks his own desire; he breaks out against all sound judgment. Proverbs 18:1 (ESV)*

- *Not neglecting to meet together, as is the habit of some, but encouraging one another, and all the more as you see the Day drawing near. Hebrews 10:25 (ESV)*

The Lord doesn't want us to be alone. He mentions this time and time again. He wants us to call on Him and those around us for help. He wants us to share our trials and our troubles with those closest to us. He wants us to find community with those who have experienced similar circumstances.

By isolating ourselves, we take away the opportunity for God to speak to us through others.

I know for certain the Lord placed people in my life not for the time when I met them, but for the time when I needed them the most – when I lost my husband Michael three years ago. He also placed new people in my path along this journey. They have been the Lord's hands and heart here on earth.

My friends and family listened night after night as I tried to process that horrific time, others helped take care of my son – who was just one and a half at the time. Another couple paid for my way to A Widow's Might conference just six weeks after Michael passed, and there were countless others who sent cards and Bible verses and words of encouragement.

God also provides us "tools" for healing. I joined a Suicide Survivors Group and sought help through counseling. Both of these tools helped fight the feeling of isolation. I could talk through my deepest darkest moments with people who could somewhat understand. I knew God was with me and I wasn't alone, but meeting others who were in a similar situation was a way the Lord showed me He was there in the midst of unbearable grief.

There are people God has and will place in your life, too. We have to be open to "hearing" them. And, that can't take place if we isolate. Sisters, I encourage you to listen, and let the Lord work in your life.

Lord, Thank You for placing people in our paths along this journey. We know it is You who ultimately provides comfort, but You also show us Your love and comfort through others on this earth. It can feel natural to isolate ourselves. But help us to connect with others and be open to listening and letting You work in our lives. Amen.

My thoughts:

_____

_____

_____

_____

_____

_____

_____

_____

_____

_____

_____

_____

_____

_____

_____

_____

_____

_____

_____

_____

△ △ △

DON'T WALK THE JOURNEY ALONE
by Kit Hinkle

Though one may be overpowered, two can defend themselves. A cord of three strands is not quickly broken.

Ecclesiastes 4:12 ESV

"Why do I have to be so alone?" she cried out over the phone after realizing that yet again, she was left off of an invite list.

I know this widow's heart for laughter and fun.

And yet I also know how awkward her friendships and social life have been since being widowed.

Have you been in this place? Feeling like your married friends don't get you? I can tell you that nearly every widow I've ministered to has experienced this.

Whether it's a neighborhood couples get together or just going out on the town with other couples it's frustrating when you have to stand-alone! At least for me, I miss having a companion to go to for encouragement when life gets lonely.

But remember the conversation at the top of this page? Guess what? That widow has me, and a network of many other widows, who understand that feeling of not having a husband by her side.

Others try to understand and help and encourage, but at some point they can't relate to not having that support physically right next to them.

And thank God they don't really get it. Because in order to be able to get it, they would have to experience the pain and loss that we've experienced. I wouldn't wish that on anyone!

So do you have your network of godly widowed women around you? Not just a network of widows or a network of Godly friends---watch the double adjective: Godly and widowed! I have lots of friends who have faith. They make wonderful friendships, and I'm thankful everyday for them. And I have lots of connections with widows--everywhere. But when I spend any significant time with a widow who doesn't walk in faith, I find out quickly that they don't have solid answers.

But the godly widowed friends--wow, they get it. And they lift me and give me suggestions when I'm struggling doing life without a husband.

You CAN build a network of like-minded ladies who get you.

I think of four ladies from Paducah, Kentucky who made a road trip to our last conference in early November.

I picture them piled into one car and headed down the highway, passing through several states. All, so that they could be filled with encouragement through Christ and meet other like-minded Christian women on this same walk of life with them.

They loved their road trip time, the laughs, the deepening of friendship bonds! They arrived and met our writer and speaker team, and laughed and told us their stories from the road. Then they met the other conference participants, and started friendships that will last forever. In fact their emails and social media chats and blog comments between these ladies and the ones they've met continue--more laughter, prayer, and encouragement. There were times during that conference that someone needed comforting.

And that's when it happened-- suddenly the new friendship filled in a hole-- because it's a friendship based on really getting it-- this walk that only widows take. And armed with knowing each other and knowing God, they both tackle issues they never thought they'd be able to tackle. A cord of three...

My thoughts:

_____

_____

_____

_____

_____

_____

_____

_____

_____

_____

_____

_____

△ △ △

WHERE DID MY FRIENDS GO?
by Kit Hinkle

Let all bitterness and wrath and anger and clamor and slander be put away from you, along with all malice. Be kind to one another, tenderhearted, forgiving one another, as God in Christ forgave you. Ephesians 4:31-32 (ESV)

A widely spoken rule of thumb says most widows lose 75% of the friendships they had before their loss.

No one can tell me where this statistic comes from, but it seems to be out there, everywhere! And when I lost Tom, I thought, no way—after all, in that first year, there was so much attention on me that I wanted to hide under a rock—seemed like everyone wanted to help me in my grief.

But gradually, through the hard road of walking alone, a year, or years out, I started to see that statistic coming true—ouch.

So with many years of widowhood behind me, I wanted to talk to you about removing any seeds of bitterness that might sprout when you notice that some of your friends might scatter.

More specifically, I want to share with you one tip: Don't always assume people say or do things (or forget to say or do things) because they are rejecting you. Try this.... List three possible reasons the person did what they did which have absolutely nothing to do with you and then simply choose one of those and decide to believe it!

"What if I'm wrong?" You might ask. "What if it IS something personal?"

Here's a truth: If you can't think of what you've done to hurt her, and she won't tell you, don't blame yourself. Many times people are mad for unfounded reasons. Many times it's their own insecurities or shame at the root of their behavior, and they are just choosing to repin it on someone else. What good does it do for you to unearth all of that?

Think of the power in that! Okay, so your friend didn't call you in your time of need. After searching yourself and owning up to your part, try some of these on for size—warning, some of these aren't necessarily excusing her actions—some reflect shallowness on her part—that isn't the point. We are all sinners, and we cannot control that even your friends are all sinners and may simply not be up for the job during this season:

•She is going through something overwhelming in her life that she doesn't want to burden you with.

•She's feeling so awful about what you're going through and doesn't have the emotional strength to walk with you through it—she's terrified and can't bear to delve into the depths with you. She feels awful about her weakness but nevertheless, it is what it is, and she can't bring herself to repair it and walk with you at the same time. It's just too much.

•She doesn't want you to see her cry.

•She's secretly feels a little to blame for your situation.

•Your situation reminds her of a painful part of her past she hasn't grappled with yet.

•She is scared to death what happened to you could happen to her, and seeing you makes her think about that—it's just too scary.

•She knows her strengths are in other areas and she's not suited for the job of lifting you through this valley.

•She's perhaps not really about helping you. Until this tragedy happened, you provided something for her that she just isn't able to get from your current situation. So she's not going to invest.

•She doesn't know what to say or do around you.

•She's afraid everything she says and does will remind you of your loss.

•She thinks you might be uncomfortable in the old circles of friends. So she's assuming you'd rather not be invited.

Even if some of the reasons may not flatter your friend, the truth is, none of these have anything to do with anything you have said and done wrong. That's what's helpful about deciding what might fit. Naturally checking in with them helps, but there are times when a friend might be too uncomfortable to discuss these with you.

Lord Father, Please give my sisters Your confidence in this season. Help her feel loved and whole in Your image. Please also give her a dose of Your mercy and enable her to forgive her sisters who have caused her pain. Help her love You by loving them. Amen

My thoughts:

_____

_____

_____

_____

_____

_____

_____

_____

_____

_____

_____

_____

_____

_____

△ △ △

Section 5: Holidays and Anniversaries

There is no getting around it, some days are just going to be hard days. Often times we start struggling a few weeks before a holiday or anniversary. What can we do to get through the tough days?

Make a plan.

A hard day can be even worse if you find yourself alone and with nothing to do. If you are the type of person who gets energy from being around others than schedule time to be with others on those days.

If you really need & want alone time then schedule a fun activity (walk in nature or try something new) for a part of the day to keep from dwelling on sad thoughts for long periods of time.

Take care of yourself.

Our feelings are often impacted by how we feel. Be intentional about getting good sleep, exercise and healthy eating particularly when you know a tough day is coming up.
Give yourself and others grace.

Even when you try to make the best of the day sometimes things go awry. Just remember to give yourself and others grace.

Create new traditions & memories.

Plan a fun activity to remember your loved one on those special days. Include others if you can!

Here are a few ideas:
- Cook their favorite meal and have family/friends over to share fun stories.
- Go to one of their favorite places.
- Serve in the community in a way that would honor them.
- Post a fun memory about them on social media and encourage others to share a memory as well.

- Do something you wouldn't normally do but your loved one loved to do.
- Do something your loved one didn't enjoy doing.
- Watch his favorite movie.
- Listen to his favorite music.
- Finish something he never finished.

EXTRAVAGANT LOVE
by Sheryl Pepple

Have you ever been loved on so much it embarrassed you? By embarrassed I mean you felt awkward, self-conscious, or ashamed. It happened to me, and it made me realize I should feel this way daily.

I have always loved Christmas. The beautiful lights, the decorations, the time with family, the parties, the music, the heart-warming movies, but most of all the wonderful celebration focused on our Savior's birth. And then came widowhood, when suddenly everything, even Christmas, seemed so different.

My first Christmas without my husband is a blank. I know my family gathered, and we went through the motions, but other than that, I have no memories of the first year.

As the second year approached, I became very anxious about how to make the second Christmas a better one. We were in so much pain, but I desperately wanted there to be some joy. So being pragmatic, I started with the decorations. I thought - well, if I just spruce up the garland it will look more festive and that will help. But

I didn't have the energy or the talent to do the sprucing up. I went to a lady at the church (someone I didn't know personally) with decorating talent and asked if she would help me spruce up the garland. She graciously accepted, and not only spruced up my garland but she transformed my home into a magical wonderland, worthy of the front cover of the most prestigious decorating magazine. It was breathtaking. And a huge sacrifice! She worked in retail, so she was working 60-80 hours a week, six days a week, and then she came over to my house and worked for many hours, every day, for over a week.

It was a magnificent gift, but the story doesn't end there. The next year God moved me to another city a five-hour drive away. And she drove to my new home and decorated it in the same magnificent fashion for our third Christmas without Dave. She was still working retail, so she would leave work, drive down, decorate non-stop for a day or two, and then drive back just in time to go to work.

This is the fifth year in a row she has done this. She has repeatedly given of her time and talents to the point she doesn't even decorate her own home. It blows my mind that someone would do this, and it embarrasses me. It is so incredible, so sacrificial...it's extravagant.

I have learned to recognize this gift for what it is – a powerful example of Christ's love, which is extravagant beyond comprehension. His love pierces the layers of protective coating I have put around my battered heart and breathes new life into me. It makes me want to shout from the rooftops... God's love isn't limited to just what's practical, it isn't limited to what we deserve, it isn't even limited to what we can comprehend, GOD'S LOVE IS EXTRAVAGANT!

God has given us the best example of all time of His extravagant love. It started that very first Christmas.

For God so loved the world, that he gave his only Son, that whoever believes in him should not perish but have eternal life. John 3:16 ESV

My thoughts:

△ △ △

A HAPPY FATHER'S DAY?
by Liz Anne Wright

Praise be to the God and Father of our Lord Jesus Christ, the Father of compassion and the God of all comfort, who comforts us in all our troubles, so that we can comfort those in any trouble with the comfort we ourselves receive from God. 2 Corinthians 1:3-4 (NIV)

Father's Day. Any way you slice it, this can be a tough holiday as a widow...especially a widow with children. The fewer years you are into this journey, the harder this day seems to be.

During the end of May, we started getting questions on the website and social media page about how to handle this important, yet often painful, day.

Dear sisters, you are not alone! Just like you, those of us on the writing team have to deal with this holiday...and all its implications and ramifications. We on the writing team for A Widow's Might each have our own opinions and traditions...ways to help make it a good or at least a passable day for us.

We would like to share some of our ideas with you.

We pray that our own traditions and methods may give you ideas on how to deal with your own Father's Day. We pray that God will be glorified, not only by what we do for Father's Day, but by your Father's Day as well.

So...here, in a slightly different format, we present our ideas. May they bless you! We will be praying for all of you on this all-important, but tough, day.

Kit: I have always believed Father's Day to be particularly important for children who have lost their father--why? Because it's an opportunity for the surviving mother to recall for them the elements of who their daddy was--those particular elements that model Christ for them. Children who grow up without a daddy run the risk of having trouble identifying with a Father God Whom they can trust. We who recognize this and can get our emotions under control enough can minister intentionally to our children with the purpose of filling in those blanks of what Dad means to them...which leads to what does God mean to them. For me with boys, I've intentionally used Father's Day to turn it into Brother's Day-- using that day to write a letter to each boy recalling over the past year the ways I've seen them grow and mature into the

Christ-like man that Dad was. That not only gives them recognition and something to look forward to, but also reinforces the parts of Dad that model Christ for them.

Linda: The first Father's Day for us came about a month after my husband passed. My daughter suggested she and I spend some time together – we went and got some frozen yogurt and shared memories about him. The second Father's Day was a bit easier – she decided to spend the day alone using all of his power tools to build a piece of furniture – and that gave me such joy – knowing that she had inherited her dad's talent and was using those tools on that particular day! As the initial raw pain of my loss is beginning to subside, the wonderful memories of specific occurrences are starting to surface. I have been giving some thought to writing those out and presenting them to my daughter at some point – perhaps next Father's Day.

Rene: We have kept Father's Day low key. The first year after John's death, the boys did each make a small gift for their dad that we took out and laid on his headstone. Then we went to lunch somewhere we thought he would have liked.

Nancy: Last year was our first without Mark. We stayed home from church. Seems like everywhere we went, there were huge banners proclaiming sales for dads, cards, etc. It was tough. We hibernated for the day, just being together the three of us. This year, I've asked the boys to think about what they want to do to celebrate. My younger son wants to get balloons to release to heaven for his dad. I will encourage them to attach notes to them, and we will read them aloud before releasing.

Liz Anne: On this day that honors fathers, we instead choose to focus on what we do have, not what we have lost. And that is truly a lot! Every year since Keith died, my boys have figured out cards for the men at church whom God has convicted to be part of our lives. Last year's card said, "As a father figure, you've nailed it." and we included a nail in the cards. We passed out upwards of 18 cards, and probably could have used a few more. The boys get really excited, dashing around church looking for each of the men. They welcome them with a big hug and present the cards. They even fight over who gets to give cards to which man. The men were touched. One of our friends even got a bit teary, as did I a few times.

My thoughts:

_____

_____

_____

_____

_____

_____

_____

_____

_____

_____

_____

_____

_____

_____

_____

_____

_____

_____

_____

_____

_____

△ △ △

NEW TRADITIONS
by Jill Byard

For everything there is a season, and a time for every matter under heaven: Ecc 3:1 ESV

Until recently in my widowhood journey, the thought of losing our traditions and changing the "way we always did things" terrified me. I believe the reason partly comes from how I lost my husband. There were no goodbyes, no preparations--he was gone in an instant. The other reasons have more to do with not wanting to forget what David means to me and what he means to our three girls. I want his life to count for something worthy of our remembering. I feel very strongly about being the torch bearer for his legacy; I try to honor God and him as I go about life.

Time slips by so quickly and it's hard to believe I have experienced four New Year Eve's without my husband. I miss his silly remarks about "not kissing me for a whole year," and reminiscing together about our first date twenty-six years ago on New Year's Eve. I miss him terribly and I enjoy soaking in those memories until I have raisin-like fingers. The memories help ease the lonely and give a much needed break from living life without my spouse.

In the last few months I have come to realize the importance and the necessity of venturing out and establishing new traditions for our little family. All four of us are living and breathing and those are the only requirements needed to know our Heavenly Father has a plan for each of us. It isn't realistic to try to stop traditions from growing when those experiences shape us and strengthen us. Being pliable is essential as we move forward. Adding some new traditions or setting aside some old ones is something the living have to consider.

So I decided to add a new tradition this year to our Christmas festivities. This gave a great source of anticipation and the planning kept me occupied. The planning wasn't too complicated, which made it as low stress as possible. As I was carrying out my plan I came to realize that this little step forward didn't take away from our memories of past Christmases, but it honored my husband in a new way. The daddy of our three girls and my husband would never, ever want his death to stop his girls from living and carrying out God's plans. He never practiced living life based on fear and didn't want anything to impede his girls from doing whatever they set out to accomplish. Bittersweet moments did shadow me through our new tradition, but the benefits and the wonderful time spent with our girls encourages me to keep working through the uneasiness.

Sweet Sisters, I want to encourage you to try out new experiences as you maneuver on this road of widowhood. The new experience will bring a little bit of excitement and a break from all the added responsibilities. Every step you take will propel you farther down the road to living out God's plan for you.

Dear Heavenly Father, Thank You for always guiding us into Your plan. Thank You for encouraging us as we try and move forward in the midst of our sorrow. We are grateful to know You take every step forward with us and You cushion our feet. In Your Mighty Name, Amen

My thoughts:

△ △ △

FIX YOUR EYES ON WHAT IS UNSEEN
by Jennifer Stanton Boswell

I brought you flowers today. Stargazer Lilies. The same flowers you always gave me.

Except you weren't there. It was just the place where your body lies.

I can never quite prepare myself for the emotional impact this day has after my husband Michael's death. Just shy of seven years of marriage when he made his way to Heaven, April 19 would have been our tenth wedding anniversary.

The date that was once filled with happiness and hope is now covered in sadness. Our anniversary is a reminder of what will never be, filled with indescribable loneliness, as the only person this day has any real significance to is not here.

It's easy to get bogged down in grief on days like this. No matter the amount of time that has passed, the memories – the "what ifs" and "what could have beens" seem to rear their heads even more. We can focus on sadness and sorrow far more than the beautiful memories and hope we have in seeing our beloved again.

At the cemetery that day, I sat sobbing, trying to find the strength to get off my knees. Anger enveloped me – "Why are you not here? Why can't you be here to see Ty grow up?" I said aloud, "God help me."

I wasn't sure how I would get up and step forward, let alone face the rest of my day. It was a burden I could not bear ... on my own.

And those are the moments I lean hard into Jesus. His strength pulled me up that day. His strength has and continues to keep me going in this life, not just surviving but thriving.

When we fix our eyes on our circumstances, they will always, always seem too heavy to bear. But when we focus on our Lord and eternal life with Him, we realize these "momentary troubles" are only temporary. This truth is what keeps me going.

Therefore we do not lose heart. Though outwardly we are wasting away, yet inwardly we are being renewed day by day. For our light and momentary troubles are achieving for us an eternal glory that far outweighs them all. So we fix our eyes not on what is seen, but on what is unseen, since what is seen is temporary, but what is unseen is eternal. 2 Corinthians 4:16-18 (NIV)

After several minutes, I stood up. Though the grief doesn't disappear, I know Jesus is with me and will continue to guide my steps no matter the circumstances this life brings.

Lord, our circumstances can seem too heavy at times – the pain can be too much. But remind us that they are only temporary and will be worth it all when we see Your face. Continue to guide our steps and help us to do Your will. Amen.

My thoughts: _____
_____
_____
_____
_____
_____
_____

△ △ △

Section 6: Waves of Grief

Blessed are those
who mourn,
for they shall
be comforted.

Matthew 5:4 ESV

WHAT DOES HE WANT?
by Bonnie Vickers

"The Lord is my portion," says my soul, "therefore I will hope in him." The Lord is good to those who wait for him, to the soul who seeks him.

Lamentations 3: 24-25 ESV

It started out as a simple trip to the grocery store.

Six weeks had passed since my husband's home going, and I could not postpone the trip any longer. I had to get some food in my house.

Carefully, I made my way through the produce section. It seemed safe enough. I even managed to make it up and down a few aisles.

So far, so good, I convinced myself.

But, as I rounded the corner, my eye caught the display of cereals--the melt down began. Struggling for air, the tears began to slowly fall. My mind took me back to the previous shopping trips, and I realized then how they were centered around my husband.
What would he want for dinner?

What kind of cereal would he want?
What would he want?

Overcome with emotions, I fled from the store.

Thankfully, by God's grace I have grown quite a bit since that grocery store melt down. Facing this new season of my life with hope and keeping my eyes focused on the cross, my question has now changed to "What would HE want?" What would GOD want?

Isn't it wonderful that He has given us a guidebook for instruction?

His Word tells us what He wants and, by delving into it, we can discover not only what He wants for our lives, but what He has in store for our lives.

What does He want? He wants us to know His...

Love
Because your steadfast love is better than life, my lips will praise you. So I will bless you as long as I live; in your name I will lift up my hands. (Psalm 63:3-4 ESV)

Comfort

You shall weep no more. He will surely be gracious to you at the sound of your cry. As soon as he hears it, he answers you. (Isaiah 30:19 ESV)

Presence
And the Lord will guide you continually and satisfy your desire in scorched places and make your bones strong; and you shall be like a watered garden, like a spring of water, whose waters do not fail. (Isaiah 58:11 ESV)

Help
Our soul waits for the Lord; he is our help and our shield. For our heart is glad in him, because we trust in his holy name.(Psalm 33:20-21 ESV)

Listening ears
In my distress I called upon the Lord; to my God I cried for help. From his temple he heard my voice, and my cry to him reached his ears. (Psalm 18:6 ESV)

Plan
For I know the plans I have for you, declares the Lord, plans for welfare and not for evil, to give you a future and a hope. (Jeremiah 29: 11 ESV)

Sisters, I know this journey is hard. But, if we trust Him - we can discover His plan for this new life we are in.

Even as we walk it without our beloved husbands by our sides.

As He cheers me on - I can imagine my husband cheering me on as well. He would be proud that I am moving forward.

We lived abundant lives with our husbands. We can now live it without them.

After all, it is what **He** wants.

Heavenly Father, Please keep our hearts and thoughts focused on Your will for this new season of our lives. Thank You for Your word where we can be assured of Your love and concern for us. Bless all these widows who search for what You want for them. Amen

My thoughts:

_____

_____

_____

_____

_____

_____

_____

_____

_____

_____

_____

_____

_____

_____

_____

_____

_____

_____

_____

_____

△ △ △

WAVES OF GRIEF
by Lori Reynolds Streller

My soul is weary with sorrow; strengthen me according to your word. ~Psalm 119:28 niv

Have you experienced intense grief in your lifetime? Maybe your family has been split apart by divorce or addiction. Possibly life has careened out of control due to a loss of income; failed infertility attempts; or sorrow in an adoption journey. You may have lost a loved one to death.

Grief attacks us in so many ways. None are immune.

Grief is as individual as we are. and there is no limit on the amount of time we spend being tossed amongst its powerful waves.

We may not have control over our grief, but we do have the power to make some important choices in the process.

There is "good grief" that brings about healing and keeps us participating in life; and there is "bad grief" that traps our thoughts into a "victimization" mentality. Both types will crash over us and pull us under. Both will change us, but only one will improve us. We must choose carefully.

We can allow the waves of grief to crash on our heads and push us out away from shore.

The more we fight their undertow, the farther out we are pushed. Thinking that we don't have to deal with the grief begins a vicious cycle. Fighting its existence will leave us in a solitary battle clinging to bitterness and self-pity; hoping for someone to rescue us, but resisting their help just the same.

Or
We can allow the strong current of grief to crash on our heads, push us under and dump us onto the shore in a heap, where although we will find ourselves at our destination, we will arrive out of breath and sputtering up water from our lungs. This arrival leaves us beat up, weak and exhausted, face first in the gritty sand.

Or
We can ride the grief waves as they come, turning to the shore in their approach. Throw our whole being into the power and fluidity of the water;

float to the top and propel forward. This option allows the grief to wash over us, but not to pull us under its powerful grip for too long. The wave will push us to the safety of the shore; we glide in its presence. It gets ahold of just enough of us to move us smoothly to safety.

I don't know the particulars of your personal loss that has brought the waves of grief upon you; but I am very familiar with what grief can do to us. It can leave us gasping for air and physically exhausted. We can cause us to lose our sense of direction.

It can also be used by God to heal us, to strengthen our faith and to mature us. This, riding the waves of grief requires we lean heavily into Jesus as our guide and stability. When we learn to grieve free of bitterness, we enable God to use our pain for His glory.

Lord, take my weary, sorrow filled soul and strengthen me according to Your word. Remind me to turn to You when the waves seem insurmountable so I can grieve in a good way; use my grief to push me closer to Your side. Amen.

My thoughts:

△ △ △

WAIT FOR IT
by Sheryl Pepple

Wait for it. But the "it" is not what you think.

As widows, we are led to believe that we must "wait" to be reunited with our husbands in heaven. We feel as they have been taken from us, and we have been left all alone to wait for years, possibly decades, for that great reunion. It makes sense. It is a logical progression of how we see time. But it is not the full picture.

Here is what I know to be true from scripture:

So then you are no longer strangers and aliens, but you are fellow citizens with the saints and members of the household of God, built on the foundation of the apostles and prophets, Christ Jesus himself being the cornerstone, in whom the whole structure, being joined together, grows into a holy temple in the Lord.

Ephesians 2:19-21 ESV

Throughout scripture we are told we are one body, with Christ as the head. Never does it separate those who are in heaven from those who are on Earth. We are one. Not as husband and wife, but as something so much more...we are one as the body of Christ.

Our minds struggle to grasp this truth. It is contrary to the way we tend to view death. But it also helps me understand a few other things, like why I feel a closer sense of connection to my husband when I am worshipping God.

Recently I was able to go on a three-week trip to Africa. As the departure date grew closer, my fears began to grow. I dreaded taking the trip without my husband. I finally decided to go – because of you. I wanted to be able to encourage you that you can do things without your husbands. I wanted you to not feel limited in this "new normal." When I came back from my trip, I eagerly shared with many how great it was to overcome my fears and to see the animals.

What I didn't share was how intensely I felt my husband's presence. One minute, I would be worshipping God our creator and in the next moment I'd be visualizing my husband beside me commenting on what we were seeing together. It's been six years since my husband went to heaven so it puzzled me to have such intense feelings of connection. I tried to rationalize it by writing it off to just strong memories. But it really didn't feel like memories. It felt like something happening in the present.

Wait for it...

This week singing in church, I again felt this intense sense of my husband's presence. Not because of the words of the song or the thoughts I was having; it was just a sense that my husband was with me, worshipping also. I was very puzzled about what triggered those feelings. Then in the communion prayer, I heard the words "we are sharing communion with the church past, present and future." His words sank in - we are actively sharing communion with the church of ALL time.

Wait for it...

The temptation to rationalize or dismiss thoughts that don't fit our traditional viewpoints is very strong. But God makes Himself known to us. We just need to be open to receive His truth. We need to have a child-like faith. While I was worshipping in service, my four year old grandson was asked in Sunday school what he was grateful for. His reply, "My grandpa, Dave-- I never got to meet him but I'm thankful for him." It doesn't make sense that this is what was on my young grandson's mind, that day, at that time. We hadn't even spoken of Dave recently. I know it was further confirmation of God's presence and the presence of His church, past, present and future – including the presence of our loved ones in the here and now.

The it...

We are one body, living and functioning, with Christ as the head. We are a part, our husbands are a part, the church of the past is a part, the church of the present is a part, the church of the future is a part. Meditate on this truth and let it permeate your heart. It is amazing.

My thoughts:

_____

_____

_____

_____

_____

_____

_____

△ △ △

GOD WILL MAKE A WAY
by Bonnie Vickers

My soul is cast down within me; therefore I remember you
Psalm 42:6 ESV

Blind-sided. Once again. Suddenly, it happened. You know that moment when something triggers 'the button'. The button that explains the "why" I am sitting alone. The button that can release a flood of memories at any given moment. The one you do your best not to press. In the midst of the church pews, I became aware that I was surrounded by couples. Husband and wives coming together to worship. And as I observed these couples and saw them sitting there with hands entwined or the husband's hand placed in the small of his wife's back, my focus was rocked. My mind retreated to the numerous times I was able to worship God along side my husband. And at that moment, my mind slipped to memories passed.

I was attending a special Sunday night meeting of prayer and music at my church. The service was well attended by many in the community, and I was truly enjoying the music and fellowship with other Christians. I was certainly not prepared for the triggered memory of worshiping alongside my husband to be stirred so deeply.

For the next few minutes, I disengaged to that place of memories. I remembered the times I was able to sit beside my husband in a church pew. I thought of all the "acts of service" that we did side by side as working laymen for the church. Pictures flashed through my mind of the many activities we were part of in serving God through work at the church. And at that moment – I so badly wanted my husband beside me. I felt such a void. It occurred to me that "worshiping together" was truly one of the biggest things I missed.

And, as the congregation stood to sing, "God Will Make A Way", I must confess to you, I could not stand. My body suddenly felt heavy, and I felt I did not have the strength to stand. So. I sat. And listened. My head was bowed and my eyes were closed. And I listened.

My soul is cast down within me; therefore I remember You.

Yes. Yes. A thousand times, yes. I remember You. I remember the many times You have consoled my grieving heart. I remember the times You have guided me through decisions that needed to be made. I remember how faithful You have been in providing for me and my girls. I remember You.

And as my blurred memories began to fade (not go away, mind you, but fade) and my focus cleared and shifted back to Him, I quietly stood and joined the singing congregation.

God will make a way for us when life's events trigger "buttons" of despair. He is the one who makes my heart worship again. And it is Him who gives me strength when I feel depleted.

Memories can be bittersweet. But, the memory of worshiping alongside my husband is so very sweet in my heart. And as I choose to continue to serve and worship God, I give Him thanks for the special times I was able to share with my husband.

He will be my guide, hold me closely by His side. With love and strength for each new day. He will make a way.

Father, how blessed we are to have You hold us so closely by Your side. I pray each widow reading these words can feel

Your love and strength to carry them through each day. Amen

My thoughts:

_____

_____

_____

_____

_____

_____

_____

_____

_____

_____

_____

_____

_____

_____

_____

_____

_____

_____

$\triangle \ \triangle \ \triangle$

Section 7: Gratitude

His Steadfast Love Endures Forever

Make a joyful noise to the LORD, all the earth!
Serve the LORD with gladness!
Come into his presence with singing!
Know that the LORD, he is God!
It is he who made us, and we are his;
we are his people, and the sheep
of his pasture.
Enter his gates with thanksgiving,
and his courts with praise!
Give thanks to him; bless his name!
For the LORD is good;
his steadfast love endures forever,
and his faithfulness to all generations.

Psalm 100: 1-5 ESV

A MORE GRATEFUL HEART
by Sheryl Pepple

For although they knew God, they did not honor Him as God or give thanks to Him, but they became futile in their thinking, and their foolish hearts were darkened.

Romans 1:21 ESV

Is it okay to be angry with God? It is a much-debated topic amongst Christians with no easy answer. Personally, I tend to lean towards one answer, but I can also see the validity in the other response. One thing I do know - staying angry with God can be hazardous to our well-being.

When we stay angry with God, we are in essence saying we don't like what He did (or didn't do). We become stuck in believing our way would have been better. Our view of Him has shifted, and we are no longer acknowledging who He really is. We are questioning either His sovereignty or His goodness or His love. We are putting our thoughts, our desires, our understanding above His. Paul warned the church in Romans 1:21 (ESV) that when we fail to worship Him or give thanks, it leads to futile thinking and darkened hearts.

Giving thanks to God can help us release our anger and help us draw closer to Him. Even science confirms the importance of gratitude. In the last decade there have been numerous studies done in the medical community citing proof that gratitude is good for our physical, emotional, and mental health. (Harvard Health Publications/Harvard Medical Health Letter/In Praise of Gratitude, Nov. 2011)

In the early days of my grief when I was consumed by my loss, I sometimes found it difficult to have a grateful heart. God helped me through that struggle by literally opening a window for my heart to feel gratitude again.

Two weeks after my husband was killed, I returned to work. It was a major effort each day to get out of bed and show up. While I was very fortunate to work at a church at the time, filled with compassionate and loving people, I found it very challenging to see my pain reflected on the faces of hundreds of people every day. Everyone knew what I was going through and there was nowhere for me to hide.

As a coping mechanism, I started rewarding myself for facing another day by going to a local drive thru for a caffeinated beverage. Every morning when the drive thru window opened, I was greeted by a wonderful young woman named Jennifer with the most beautiful smile, full of joy, and thankfully unaware of the pain I was in. Jennifer worked the same schedule I did, Sunday –Thursday. She never missed a day and she never hesitated in giving me a joyful smile. Her smile became a treasured gift given day after day, week after week, for over two years. Her smile reminded my heart of His goodness and His love. It opened my heart back up to acknowledging God and giving thanks for the simple things He provides all along the way, even in the most difficult seasons.

Scripture reminds us repeatedly to be grateful. Not just because He deserves it, but also because it is what is best for us. Are you trying to find ways to have a more grateful heart? Ask God for help and perhaps a close trusted friend who can help point those things out.

Dear Heavenly Father, You are our Sovereign Lord who deserves praise and worship. You are a mighty God who loves us always. Lord, create in us a more grateful heart. Amen.

My thoughts:

_____

_____

_____

_____

_____

_____

_____

_____

_____

_____

_____

_____

_____

_____

_____

_____

_____

_____

_____

_____

△ △ △

KALEIDOSCOPE VISION
by Sheryl Pepple

Do you still not see or understand? Are your hearts hardened? Do you have eyes but fail to see, and ears but fail to hear? And don't you remember? Mark 8:17-18 NIV

Harsh words!

Jesus rebuked the disciples because they failed to understand the meaning of His presence with them. They saw things from a human perspective, just what things looked like on the surface. They missed the bigger picture, the kingdom perspective.

How often do we do the same?

A couple of weeks ago I was out doing some last minute Christmas shopping. It was taking longer than expected, due to some road construction. Traffic was backed up for quite a while, but I was patient. The next day I had to do my grocery shopping. I didn't worry about road construction since it was in a different direction than I had traveled the day before.

SURPRISE, now they were working in that direction as well. I maintained my cool, but wondered – who plans to start multiple road construction projects in the same area, right before the holidays?

Finally, I was done with my errands and my Christmas shopping. The next day was Sunday and I planned a nice quiet day at home after church. I headed out at my usual time and yep, you guessed it, I encountered yet another new construction project. As I sat in the backed up traffic, I prided myself on the fact that I wasn't demonstrating outright road rage at this point, because I HATE getting to church late.

Once again, I found myself pondering how anyone could do such poor planning regarding road construction projects. All I could "see" was the inconvenience to me. As I sat there, I watched the crew repeatedly pouring the hot tar and smoothing it out. Oh and the awful smell of that tar, I couldn't imagine having to do a job that smelled so awful.

Eventually, my thoughts began to shift and I started to see things from a totally different perspective. It was like I had been looking through a kaleidoscope and the pieces had suddenly shifted into a beautiful new pattern. I began to see that the workers were not an annoyance, but they were servants who were serving. They were serving the community and serving me by performing a job that I couldn't do, and wouldn't want to do on my best day.

My heart started to fill with gratitude. I began thanking God for the workers and for providing them to serve. Thanking Him for being sovereign over everything – even the schedule of road construction projects.

Thanking Him for living in me and bringing me back to a place of peace and gratitude. I was grateful for being reminded we often get trapped in seeing things from a human perspective, and it is a tremendous blessing when we see, hear, and remember the bigger picture, the kingdom perspective. He not only provides for our immediate needs, He brings us peace and Eternal Life. That is what He wanted His disciples to see then and it is what He wants His followers to see today! I pray that as we enter this holiday season our vision will shift to a kingdom perspective and our hearts will be overflowing with gratitude.

Dear Heavenly Father, We praise You and worship You! Thank You for You! Let Your will be done on earth as it is in heaven! We thank You for the gift of Your Son that we may have peace and Eternal Life! Help us to see, hear, and remember You. In Your Son's Holy and Precious Name! Amen.

My thoughts:

_____

_____

_____

_____

_____

_____

_____

_____

_____

_____

_____

_____

_____

_____

△ △ △

ENOUGH
by Bonnie Vickers

Draw near to God, and he will draw near to you. James 4:8 ESV

I am quite sure we all have our "list".

A list of events, both good and bad, that have certainly shaped our lives.

Events that have brought us joy and satisfaction.

Events that have brought sadness and pain.

It is easy to reflect on the good list. Times we are grateful for God's goodness to us. Times we can sing praises of thanksgiving and trust He is enough.

But, what about the bad list? The list of events we simply wish we could erase and dispose? Times we struggle to sing praises of thanksgiving and truly trust He is enough.

Where do we stand then?

Trust me when I say it has taken me years of struggles, tears and hard knocks to say, "Jesus is Enough."

I have been through enough to KNOW He is enough for me.

As a very young adult, I watched my father fight an incurable disease that ended his life at fifty-six. Later, I saw the ravages of Alzheimer attack my mother at the age of sixty-seven and succumb to health issues at sixty-nine. And most notable, watching my husband, my helpmate and best friend make every effort to fight the earthly disease of cancer invading his body. It was a disease which destroyed his earthly vessel at the young age of fifty-three. These make up parts of my bad list. And, as stated earlier, we all have one. A list is not used for comparison to anyone else's, just my own. In the end, however, we feel some of the same emotions; great sadness, loss and abandonment.

What exactly turned my cries from "Why, Lord?" to "Lord, You are enough"? It simply lies in the proof of His faithfulness in carrying me these past four years, He walked with me through the valley of grief and despair as I mourned over the loss of my husband, mother and father. He has carried me through the fear and loneliness where no one else could.

In the beginning, my focus was on what I did not have. At fifty years old, I no longer had my spouse beside me to share life with. Nor did I have a parent to help support my role as a single parent. My focus was on what was missing. I wrestled with Him pleading my case of how this certainly could not be for good. I reminded Him how I had served Him in church positions and in tithing. I cried out "Why?" and "Where are you?" too many times to count.

Thankfully, sisters, I now share a different tone. My focus has shifted to what I do have. And I fall to my knees in gratitude over the numerous ways He has cared for me these past four years. He has shown up in so many ways. Answered prayers. Unexpected blessings. Assurance of His presence. He has delivered both small and big things! He has been so faithful through these turbulent years. These struggles that are so raw and hurtful have lead me to total surrender and trust. I must remind myself to not focus on my circumstances. As much as I do not like them, I must remember, above all else, that God loves me. I must let contentment of His love wash over me. And yes, I do know it is sometimes easier said than done. Our walk as widows is a very difficult and individual journey.

Some of you, I have met. Most I have not. I pray for each of you, widows throughout the universe, to find this place of contentment. I pray for the day when you also can say, I have been through enough to KNOW He is enough.

My thoughts: _____

_____

_____

_____

_____

_____

_____

_____

_____

_____

_____

△ △ △

We would like to thank our AWM writing team, past and present, for contributing to this devotional.

Sheryl Pepple, President and Director
Elizabeth Dyer Colvard, Director
Kit Hinkle, Advisory Board Member
Erika Graham
Janene Gaynor
Terri Oxner Sharp
Lori Reynolds Streller
Jennifer Stanton Boswell
Ami Akins Wickiser
Jill Byard
Bonnie Vickers
Leah Stirewalt
Karen Emberlin
Katie Hagan
Linda Lint
Liz Anne Wright
Rene Zonner
Nancy Howell

A Widow's Might, Inc.

OTHER BOOKS BY A WIDOW'S MIGHT, INC.

For the Love of Her Life (summer)

For the Love of Her Life (autumn)

For the Love of Her Life (winter)

For the Love of Her Life (spring)

Made in the USA
Monee, IL
11 April 2023